The Inner Structure of Tai Chi

Mastering the Classic Forms of Tai Chi Chi Kung

Mantak Chia and Juan Li

Destiny Books
Rochester, Vermont

Destiny Books
One Park Street
Rochester, Vermont 05767
www.InnerTraditions.com

Destiny Books is a division of Inner Traditions International

Library of Congress Cataloging-in-Publication Data

Chia, Mantak, 1944-
The inner structure of tai chi : mastering the classic forms of tai chi chi kung /
Mantak Chia and Juan Li.
p. cm.
Includes bibliographical references and index.
ISBN 978-159477058-6
1. Qi gong. 2. Tai chi. I. Li, Juan. II. Title.
RA781.8.C4694 2005
613.7'148–dc22
2005018037

Printed and bound in the United States by Versa Press, Inc.

10 9 8 7 6 5

Text design and layout by Priscilla Baker
This book was typeset in Janson, with Present and Futura used as display typefaces

Contents

Acknowledgments

The Universal Tao Publications staff extend our gratitude to the many generations of Taoist Masters who have passed on their special lineage, in the form of an oral transmission, over thousands of years. We thank Taoist Master I Yun (Yi Eng) for his openness in transmitting the formulas of Taoist Inner Alchemy. We also thank Wu-style Tai Chi Master Edward Yee, who taught Master Chia the complete Tai Chi system; Tai Chi Master P. Y. Tam for the teaching of Tai Chi Chi Kung; and Master Cheng Yao-Lun for his teachings of Changing the Tendons and Sinews and Washing the Bone Marrow.

We offer our special thanks to Juan Li for his fine illustrations and for his preparation of the original draft of the first half of the manuscript. As always, he has played an integral role in presenting the Universal Tao concepts and techniques.

We express our deep appreciation to Jampa Mackenzie Stewart for his writing contributions and for his overall help in organizing and editing the first edition of this book, and we also thank Judith Stein, Kimberly Baldt, Dennis Lewis, Gary Oshinsky, Karl Danskin, Lynnette Brooks, and Michael Manelis for their assistance in editing and producing that edition. A special thank-you also goes to Saysunee Yongyod, photographer; Udon Jandee, illustrator; and Raruen Keawpadung for computer graphics.

We also wish to thank our editors at Inner Traditions, Susan Davidson and Vickie Trihy, as well as designer Priscilla Baker, for their valuable contributions to this new edition of *Inner Structure of Tai Chi*.

We offer our eternal gratitude to our parents and teachers for their many gifts to us. Remembering them brings joy and satisfaction to our continued efforts in presenting the Universal Tao System. As always, their contribution has been crucial in presenting the concepts and techniques of the Universal Tao. We wish to thank the thousands of unknown men and women of the Chinese healing arts who developed many of the methods and ideas presented in this book.

v

Putting Tai Chi Chi Kung into Practice

As you will read in the first chapter of this book, Tai Chi was originally developed as a martial art, with offensive and defensive movements. Nowadays Tai Chi is most often practiced as a moving meditation; in the Universal Tao practice of Tai Chi we focus on strengthening the internal body.

The practices described herein have been used for thousands of years by Taoists trained by personal instruction. When Tai Chi is practiced as a martial art, the degree of damage visited on one's opponent can range from harmless to lethal. The reader should practice movements taught in this book with great care and should not undertake these practices without also receiving personal instruction from a certified instructor of the Universal Tao. Universal Tao instructors can be located at our Web sites: www.universal-tao.com and www. taoinstructors.org.

The practices described herein are *not* intended to be used as an alternative or substitute for professional medical treatment and care. If a reader is suffering from a mental or emotional disorder, he or she should consult with an appropriate professional health care practitioner or therapist. Such problems should be corrected before one starts training. People who have high blood pressure, heart disease, or a generally weak condition should proceed cautiously, having received prior consent from a qualified medical practitioner.

The Universal Tao and its staff and instructors cannot be responsible for the consequences of any practice or misuse of the information in this book. If the reader undertakes any exercise without strictly following the instructions, notes, and warnings, the responsibility must lie solely with the reader.

Foreword

JAMPA MACKENZIE STEWART, OMD
SENIOR UNIVERSAL TAO INSTRUCTOR

I had been practicing and teaching Tai Chi for about ten years when I first met Master Mantak Chia in 1982. I had already learned Old Chen style, Yang style, Wu style, Cheng Man-Ching style, and Twenty-Four style Tai Chi. In fact, I knew so many different Tai Chi forms that I could not practice them all in one day.

For years I had read books about the mysterious inner changes that were supposed to take place as a result of Tai Chi practice—transforming sexual energy into chi and chi into spirit. Yet the Tai Chi teachers I studied with either didn't know about these practices or wouldn't divulge their knowledge. While I practiced hard what I had been taught, I was frustrated by the snail's pace at which I seemed to be progressing. I was elated to finally find Mantak Chia, a true Taoist master who was openly teaching the esoteric secrets of Taoist inner alchemy.

Still, the last thing I wanted to learn was another Tai Chi form! When I first saw Master Chia's Tai Chi Chi Kung form, there seemed to be nothing to it—only Grasping the Bird's Tail and Single Whip. I already knew five different ways of doing these movements. I was therefore able to learn Master Chia's form in one day. Or so I thought.

I was quite proud of my Tai Chi when I went to the Catskill Mountains in upstate New York for Master Chia's teacher training retreat in the summer of 1986. Master Chia required that all his instructors learn Tai Chi Chi Kung as a prerequisite for teaching the higher-level practices of the Universal Tao. "No sweat," I thought. "My years of prior training will stand me in good stead."

What a rude and humiliating awakening I was in for! Master Chia was merciless with me and brutally frank in his assessment of my Tai Chi. "You barely passed," he told me. "How can you practice Tai Chi for so many years and still have no root?" Each successive year thereafter he would say to me,

"You still don't get it! No spinal cord power. No spiraling. If you teach Tai Chi you have to know these things."

How could there be so much to master in so short a form?

It slowly dawned on me, through the veils of my stubborn pride and tenacious ignorance, that Tai Chi has nothing to do with the number of moves one learns or the different styles one knows—it's the quality of each movement that counts. When a student understands the profound principles of body mechanics, energy transfer, and mental focus that have been preserved within Tai Chi from the earliest masters down to the present, then everything that student does is Tai Chi. On the other hand, if you don't grasp the principles of inner structure, then although your Tai Chi movements may look beautiful, your form is empty and hollow.

Western boxing has only about five techniques, yet consider how difficult it is to become a champion boxer like Muhammad Ali or Mike Tyson. Tai Chi has thirteen basic techniques as well as hundreds of inner principles of movement. The simple form of Tai Chi Chi Kung contains them all.

With fewer outer movements to perform, the Tai Chi Chi Kung student quickly progresses from the initial stage of learning the outer form to the stage of mastering the inner structure of Tai Chi. I had to grudgingly admit that Master Chia's students, who had studied Tai Chi Chi Kung with him for only three intensive weeks, were further along than my students who had studied the longer Tai Chi forms over two or three years!

Most other traditional Tai Chi masters required their students to train in Tai Chi for years before they exposed them to internal energy work such as the Microcosmic Orbit Meditation. After years of devoted study and service, the master would secretly take the fortunate and diligent student into his inner sanctum and reward him by teaching him the Microcosmic Orbit as the crowning initiation in his training. Part of Master Chia's genius is his insistence that students learn the Microcosmic Orbit meditation and Iron Shirt Chi Kung at the outset, as prerequisites to Tai Chi Chi Kung.

Master Chia teaches Tai Chi as one limb of the Universal Tao system, an integrated approach to cultivating healing energy through the Tao. All the different parts of the Universal Tao system—sitting meditation, standing meditation, moving meditation, the cultivation of sexual energy, and healing work—mutually support one another. A student's progress in meditation, healing, and Chi Kung—internal energy work—is immediately reflected in his or her Tai Chi, and vice versa.

Tai Chi Chi Kung teaches us to move in harmony with the principles of the Tao. It is based on classical Taoist philosophy as presented in the I Ching, in the Tao Te Ching, in Chuang Tzu and Lieh Tzu, and in Sun Tzu's *The Art of War*. Its principles are also rooted in the esoteric Taoist teachings of inner alchemy as taught by the great immortals Ko Hung, Lu Tung-Pin, and others. The legends say it was a Taoist immortal, Chang San-Feng of Wu Tang Mountain, who originally created Tai Chi. Modern research seems to indicate it was probably a retired general of the Ming dynasty, Chen Wang-Ting, who developed Tai Chi and taught it to the people of his village as their clan's martial arts style. In any event, Chen's writings clearly show that he too was deeply steeped in esoteric Taoist inner alchemy.

Knowledge is power. In the days when warfare meant hand-to-hand combat, martial arts skills were military secrets and were not taught openly. Similarly, the esoteric methods of Taoist internal alchemical cultivation were reserved for selected and carefully screened initiates. Even in this century, that tradition of secrecy has continued to a great extent. Contemporary Tai Chi masters still have their esoteric students and their select "indoor" disciples who receive the full transmission of the art. The Chinese are so good at keeping secrets that the outer students often don't even know that they are missing anything.

Fortunately, this pattern seems to be changing. Through the openness of Master Chia and other recent masters, the proverbial cat is out of the bag. The teachings are now available for anyone who wants to take advantage of this golden opportunity to receive the sublime distillation of thousands of years of Chinese wisdom.

This book presents the first levels of the art of Tai Chi Chi Kung. Master Chia calls his form Tai Chi Chi Kung instead of the more common name, Tai Chi Chuan. *Chuan* literally means "fist" and denotes an emphasis on the use of the art for fighting. *Chi Kung* means "energy cultivation." While Chi Kung can be applied toward enhancing one's martial arts abilities, it can also be directed toward healing oneself and others and toward refining one's spirit for the realization of wisdom and inner peace.

Although martial skills are certainly a significant part of Master Chia's presentation of Tai Chi Chi Kung, in the hierarchy of importance the ability to defend oneself and secure a peaceful environment ought to be followed by the wise use of the life force one has fought to preserve. A life dedicated only to fighting seems tragic, does it not? Learning to heal ourselves and then to heal others, learning to soar into the realms of the spirit, returning to harmony with ourselves, with society, and with nature, are what we are really here to do.

Foreword

✗

Preface

Master Mantak Chia

The form described in this book is called Tai Chi Chi Kung. I have studied and practiced Tai Chi for more than thirty years now. I began by learning three different forms of Yang-style Tai Chi from five different masters. Later I learned Wu style with Master Edward Yee, and then Chen-style Tai Chi. Finally I met Master P. Y. Tam, who taught me Tai Chi Chi Kung, a very early form of the Yang style, emphasizing the use of the mind and heart to move chi. The chi in turn improves the circulation, enlivens the bone structure, and revitalizes the whole system.

The Tai Chi Chi Kung form stresses the inner structure of Tai Chi, the way chi flows in the body and the way energy is transmitted through the bone structure from the ground. This form is simple and easy to master, yet it contains all the essential movements of Tai Chi.

In the past most masters have taught 108-movement forms of Tai Chi, making the learning process extremely complicated and time consuming. In many cases it took years simply to learn the form before students could begin to explore the inner structure of Tai Chi. Using this short and essential Tai Chi Chi Kung form, the student can almost immediately begin to apply the vital principles of Tai Chi: absorbing, transforming, and directing the three forces. The three forces are the universal force, which comes from the stars, sun, and moon; the cosmic force, which comes from the cosmic particles in and around the atmosphere and environment; and the earth energy, which comes from the earth itself.

The Tai Chi principles and methods of internal power training are applicable to all styles of Tai Chi. However, Tai Chi Chi Kung must be understood, studied, and practiced within the context of Taoism; it is but one branch (albeit an important one) of a comprehensive system of Taoist practices. Each branch relies on the other branches for support. Thus, in this book there are numerous references to the Taoist meditations and Chi Kung practices that

I teach my Tai Chi students within the context of the Universal Tao system. I have already written many books describing these practices in minute and complete detail, so readers wishing in-depth information should refer to these works. However, I have also included brief descriptions of the beginning-level Universal Tao practices both in the main text and in the appendices for the benefit of new readers and students.

We wish you every success in your study and mastery of Tai Chi Chi Kung. May the chi be with you!

Introduction

China's oldest system of philosophy and spiritual practice is Taoism. Taoists observe that we are part of nature; we are born of the energy of the earth and stars and elements. Yet for some reason we forget our place in nature, and so we need to learn how to reclaim our rightful heritage as children of nature.

The way of nature is called the Tao. The way to realizing our highest potential, living in harmony with the patterns and energy of nature, is also called the Tao. To Taoists, the journey and the goal are one. Life is lived as a process, as a dance.

Just as the universe is an integrated whole, the body is an integrated whole, with each part connected to and dependent on the other parts. Yet as we become adults and begin to lead increasingly sedentary lives, we often forget to use all the parts of our bodies. We depend on the head and arms, using the spine, hips, and legs only to get us from the car to the elevator to the desk chair, where we can use the head and arms again. By restricting our movement, we forget how to move lithely, with strength and efficiency. When we forget how to live fully in our bodies we overly restrict the way we move, and eventually we forget who we really are.

Tai Chi Chi Kung is an integral part of Taoism. Based on the highest principles of the Tao, it is both an expression of the Tao through movement and a personal practice for understanding and realizing the essence of the Tao. Through daily Tai Chi Chi Kung practice we can become as children again, without stiffness or tension. We can relearn to move freely and naturally with the whole body connected, both structurally and energetically. In this way we mirror our connection to the larger whole, as part of the universe. Through Tai Chi Chi Kung we can become fully ourselves.

There are many styles of Tai Chi today. Regardless of style, the first step is to learn and remember the outer movements. When a student practices all the movements in sequence, that is called the Tai Chi form. Once a student learns the form, the rest of the work in mastering Tai Chi involves learning to use energy in each posture. Working with chi, or energy, is called internal work.

The internal work is what makes Tai Chi unique and what distinguishes it from the external forms of martial arts. The inner structure is what allows the body to move as a whole. Not learning the internal part of Tai Chi is like never bothering to look inside the oyster to find the pearl.

The foundation for mastering the internal structure of Tai Chi is energy meditation. Many Tai Chi students around the world do not receive any training in energy meditation; unfortunately, most people are taught long and difficult Tai Chi forms first. They have to go through many years of practice and correction to perfect the outer form and make it look beautiful. Because of the time devoted to the outer form, the internal work is often neglected.

The major advantage of Tai Chi Chi Kung is that it is a short form repeated in four directions. But although it is a short form, it contains the essence of the movements of the longer Tai Chi forms. Since it is repetitive it does not take long to learn, so the student can quickly proceed to the internal work. Once the student becomes familiar with the essence of Tai Chi Chi Kung, learning the long forms is relatively easy.

Lack of meditation experience, along with the need to learn lengthy forms, makes it difficult for people to go into internal work. In the Universal Tao these aspects of Tai Chi are taught separately as sitting energy meditation, standing meditation, and moving meditation.

SITTING ENERGY MEDITATION

In sitting meditation the practitioner sits in a comfortable position. Through sitting practice you can strengthen your awareness and concentration without being distracted by the body's movement. The first emphasis in this practice is to learn to quiet and focus the mind and to relax the internal organs and other specific parts of the body. This phase is accomplished through the Inner Smile and the Six Healing Sounds. For instruction in the Inner Smile and the Six Healing Sounds practices see my book *Transform Stress into Vitality*.

The next step is to connect with life energy. This is accomplished through practice of the Microcosmic Orbit and the Fusion of the Five Elements meditations, wherein the student trains the mind to feel chi; to generate and gather it into a desired energy center, the tan tien; to direct chi to other areas for healing and strengthening; and then to store the chi for future use. Through a purification process, the energy is transformed to a higher level of mental

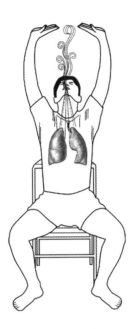

Sitting energy meditation

Standing energy meditation

quietness, balance, and inner happiness. When a student learns Tai Chi without the benefit of a sitting meditation, it is more difficult to feel chi and to use the mind's eye to gather, concentrate, and guide the energy.

STANDING ENERGY MEDITATION

After learning sitting meditation, a student will find it easier to learn standing meditations such as Iron Shirt Chi Kung. In Iron Shirt Chi Kung the practitioner gently packs, or compresses, energy and guides it through the Microcosmic Orbit. Additionally the student learns to adjust the structure of his or her stance in alignment with gravity, in order to become "grounded" or "rooted" both structurally and energetically.

Once students have the feeling of aligning and integrating the body's structure in this way while standing still, they can carry this experience into movement within the Tai Chi form. Standing meditation is the quickest and easiest way of mastering this vital internal aspect of Tai Chi. Nearly all the great Tai Chi masters acknowledge standing meditation as a major factor in their attainment of high levels of skill.

MOVING ENERGY MEDITATION

Through Tai Chi Chi Kung you can integrate what you have learned through sitting and standing meditation practice into movement. As you master the Tai Chi principles of movement, you can gradually apply these same principles in all your movements throughout daily life. Whether washing the dishes, doing yard work, or walking down the street, you will spontaneously move in harmony with the Tao. This is the essence of Tai Chi Chi Kung.

In this book, *The Inner Structure of Tai Chi*, you will first be introduced to the background, history, and basic principles of Tai Chi Chi Kung. Next, you will learn a set of simple yet powerful warm-up exercises to help open the energy centers, joints, and tendons. Following the warm-ups you will learn to feel chi through a simple standing energy meditation. After this you will be guided step by step through the Tai Chi Chi Kung form.

Because the Tai Chi Chi Kung form consists of only a few easy-to-master movements, your mind is soon free to learn how to experience and direct the chi flow.

Tai Chi is an art. As with most arts, personal instruction is essential if a student wishes to reach the highest levels. This book has two main functions: to introduce beginners to the art of Tai Chi and to help those who have already been practicing Tai Chi understand both the basic and the deeper underlying principles of what many Tai Chi masters are unwilling to speak about. While this book can be used as a handbook by those already studying Tai Chi Chi Kung with a certified Universal Tao instructor, it will also be of great value to students of other Tai Chi styles, as the principles presented apply to all styles of Tai Chi.

Once you have learned the form, chapter 6 presents different focuses for beginning- and intermediate-level practice. The rest of the book contains in-depth instruction for mastering the higher levels of all forms of Tai Chi.

If you do not have access to a certified Universal Tao instructor, you may find that having the Tai Chi Chi Kung I guided videocassette will be helpful in your practice at the beginning.

The Origins of Tai Chi Chi Kung

Archaeological discoveries during the last several decades have found ample evidence that calisthenics and breathing exercises were practiced as early as the Chou dynasty (circa 1100–221 B.C.E.). Tai Chi probably developed out of ancient forms of Tao-In and Chi Kung exercise, combined with internal circulation of energy and breath and the popular martial applications of the time.

Traditional Tai Chi histories, written after Tai Chi had become widespread, state that during the fourteenth century a Taoist hermit by the name of Chang San-Feng received the Tai Chi teachings in a series of dreams. Other

Fig. 1.1 Chang San-Feng, the legendary creator of Tai Chi

accounts assert that Chang San-Feng developed Tai Chi after observing a battle between a snake and a crane. Yet another version places Tai Chi's origins during the Tang dynasty (618–907 C.E.).

Perhaps the most credible theory is that Tai Chi was created by Chen Wang-Ting, the ninth-generation chief of the Chen family clan in Honan province. Chen Wang-Ting was a general in the army of the Ming dynasty. When the Ming dynasty fell to the Manchurians in 1644, Chen retired to Chenjiagou (Chen family village) in Honan province and used his military training to devise a series of movements to teach his clan members. The movements were based on the Red Fist style of the nearby Shaolin Temple combined with movements from the famous boxing manual of General Chi Ji-Guang.

Some accounts say that years later a wandering Taoist named Chuan Fa visited Chenjiagou and taught the Chen clan to adapt principles of the Tao (such as using the chi flow and yin and yang) into their movements, thus converting the Chen family boxing style into Tai Chi Chuan, "Supreme Ultimate" boxing. The Chen family, however, disputes these accounts, claiming Chuan Fa was merely a student of Chen Wang-Ting. The Chen family notes that it is clear from Chen Wang-Ting's early writings that he was already familiar with Taoist inner alchemy when he devised his Chen-style Tai Chi forms. It is also clear that all the other common Tai Chi styles were later derived from Chen-style Tai Chi.

Fig. 1.2 Chen family–style Tai Chi by Chen Fa-Kor (1887–1955), a descendant of the founder

Until the beginning of this century Tai Chi was considered a secret practice, passed down within the closely knit structure of family and loyal disciples. Training in the martial arts was very expensive to pursue. Accomplished masters would often demand exorbitant fees in gold bars, cash, or services. The masters expected total loyalty and obedience from the disciples. In addition, the training demanded many years of single-minded practice.

With the increasingly widespread availability and use of firearms, almost all of the martial arts styles began a rapid decline. Because firearms require very little training and practically no discipline to master, those who learned to use a gun had a distinct advantage over those who had trained arduously in martial arts. Thus the outlook seemed bleak for the martial arts at the dawn of the twentieth century. Faced with the prospect of their art becoming obsolete, some of the old masters began to teach openly to anyone who could afford it. As old Imperial China collapsed in chaos in 1912 and the experiment in a republican democracy ended with the Communist victory in 1949, martial arts made a slow transition from being a deadly art of war to becoming a health and longevity practice.

The last five decades in particular have witnessed the emergence of Tai Chi as a health practice among the masses in China. Visitors to China or any large overseas Chinese community regularly see large groups of people of all ages practicing Tai Chi outdoors in the early hours of the morning. The fascination with Tai Chi has also spread to non-Chinese communities all over the world.

Before the Second World War began, the Asian martial arts were almost totally unknown in North America. It was during the war in the Pacific that American soldiers brought back news of the extraordinary abilities of some Japanese fighters. During the occupation of Japan, many American soldiers began to study judo, jujitsu, karate, and other Japanese martial arts. Soon after the Korean war, Korean martial arts were introduced to the West as well.

From the early 1960s into the mid-1970s, the predominant forms of martial arts practiced in North America and Europe were judo, karate, aikido, and tae kwon do. Tai Chi started to capture the public's attention during the late 1960s. Since then it has continued to spread, becoming one of the most widely practiced forms of health exercise around the world.

The practice of Tai Chi, as popularized during this century, has come down to the present through three major family traditions. The first is the Chen-family style, as discussed earlier, with its combination of soft and explosive power techniques. The second is the Yang-family style, derived from the Chen style in the nineteenth century, with its smooth and even-flowing tempo. The

Fig. 1.3 Yang family–style Tai Chi by Yang Cheng-Fu (1883–1936)

Fig. 1.4 Wu family–style Tai Chi by Wu Chien-Chuan (1870–1949)

third is the Wu-family style, derived from both the Chen and Yang forms in the nineteenth century, with its subtle joint movements. Another famous but lesser-known family style is Sun style Tai Chi, a system created in the early twentieth century by the great internal-style boxer Sun Lu-Tang. This form combines elements of Hsing I Chuan and Pa Kua Chang within the Tai Chi sequence. Yet another lesser-known family system is Hao-style Tai Chi, derived from Chen style in the nineteenth century and characterized by very small and intricate circular movements. Still others are Fu-style Tai Chi and Chen Pan-Ling–style Tai Chi, both created in the twentieth century. These two are called "combined styles" because they integrate the flavor and expression of the three major family styles into their way of doing the movements. There are also other nonfamily styles, some reputedly developed in the monasteries and temples centuries ago and others created in this century. Some of these are Kuang Ping Tai Chi, Wu Tang Tai Chi, Yang's Twenty-Four style Tai Chi, and Cheng Man-Ching style (an abridged variation of the Yang-family style).

The form we explore in this book is the thirteen-movement form, which we call Tai Chi Chi Kung I. This form is believed to have originated with the Chen family. It was modified by the Yang family in the nineteenth century and has been passed down in numerous variations to the present.

Despite the multiplicity of styles and variations, the basic principles of all forms of Tai Chi are essentially the same:

1. Concentrating the mind and chi.
2. Relaxing in movement while distinguishing the full (yang) from the empty (yin).
3. Keeping the body rooted to the ground and the center of gravity low.
4. Keeping the bone structure aligned with the forces of heaven and earth and transferring the earth force through the bone structure into a single point of discharge.
5. Allowing the chi to circulate and move the muscles, bones, and tendons in slow, coordinated movements without ever pushing the physical limitations of the body to extremes and moving smoothly and continuously with total bodily integration.

The thirteen-movement style is simple in its structure, yet it encompasses the essence of Tai Chi. The form is compact enough to be practiced in a space only four feet square. Tai Chi Chi Kung is practiced to the four directions, starting with the north corner and moving counterclockwise, leading with the left hand; then returning clockwise, leading with the right hand. Because the right-side and left-side forms follow each other, the Tai Chi set can be extended for as long as one desires. If time is limited, you can simply practice the thirteen movements in just one direction.

Urban Tai Chi practitioners are often frustrated by the need to find a large private space for practicing the longer forms, which can take two to three hundred square feet of open space to do properly. Often the longer forms have so many movements that they require twenty minutes or more to complete. The thirteen-movement form is the perfect set for anyone wanting to practice Tai Chi within the time and space limitations of city life.

WU CHI

According to Taoist cosmology, before the universe was made manifest there was a state of total emptiness. In this primordial state, nothing stirred. The relative concept of time did not apply to the primordial state because there was nothing to measure time against. All was a void.

The ancient Taoists gave this state a name. They called it Wu Chi. *Wu* means "absence," "negation," "nothingness." Even though it is spelled the same way in English as the word that means life force, the *chi* in Wu Chi is a totally different word; it means "highest" or "ultimate." *Wu chi* thus means "ultimate state of nothingness."

Fig. 1.5 The empty circle symbolizes Wu Chi, the state of pure openness.

Fig. 1.6 The ever-moving dance of yin and yang is the ongoing expression of Wu Chi.

Through some unknown impulse, the Wu Chi stirred, and the first moment of creation began. This first impulse manifested as chi through the primordial polarity of yin and yang, negative and positive. The interplay of yin and yang is the essential expression of Wu Chi. The Taoists named this process Tai Chi, or "Supreme Ultimate." All the multiplicity of phenomena found in the universe, visible or invisible, are the result of yin and yang interaction.

CHI: THE SOURCE OF ALL MOVEMENT

In the same way that electricity is the foundation of modern civilization, chi, or life force, is the foundation of all the Taoist practices. Without electricity practically every aspect of our modern lifestyle comes to a stop. Similarly, without chi one's life comes to an abrupt halt.

Chi can be defined as bioelectricity, life force, vitality, or simply energy. Chi is all of these but none of them exclusively. Just as electricity is still incomprehensible to scientists in its total breadth and depth, chi is beyond intellectual understanding.

According to the ancient Taoists, chi is found in the air we breathe, yet it is not just oxygen or any of the other gaseous components of the atmosphere. Chi is also found in the food we eat, yet it is not just a vitamin, mineral, or carbohydrate that we can chemically isolate. Chi is absorbed into the food we eat through the process of photosynthesis, yet it is not sunlight or any other type of ray detectable by modern sensing devices.

Chi is the essence of the food we eat and the air we breathe—the real nourishment of the body. When we breathe or eat, we are taking chi into our bodies. Without chi, there can be no life.

FIVE ELEMENTS OR PHASES

The interaction of yin and yang is expressed through five basic phases of energy behavior, often called the Five Elements. The Five Elements refer not only to the five physical elements we find all around us but also to the five ways chi expresses itself in the universe. The first phase is energy at rest, energy in an extreme state of quietness and concentration. This phase is named *water* because water, if undisturbed, naturally becomes extremely still. The second phase is a development of the first; if energy is extremely quiet and concentrated, it bursts into activity at some point, just like the Wu Chi. This second phase is that expansion of energy. It is called *wood*, because trees burst into activity in the spring after their long period of winter rest. The burst of activity in the wood phase cannot last for long; it soon stabilizes into a period of sustained energy release. This third phase is named *fire*, because fire is able to sustain a high level of energy release over a long period. As the high energy-release rate of fire begins to decline it produces ash, giving rise to the fourth phase, *earth*. This phase of energy, the ground of all the elements, gives rise to the fifth phase, called *metal*, a very condensed state of energy that can be mined from the earth. When metal is heated it becomes molten, giving rise once again to the state of quiet concentration that is the water element.

Yin/yang is the root and trunk of all creation; the Five Elements are the branches that bear the leaves, flowers, and fruits of the universe. The result of

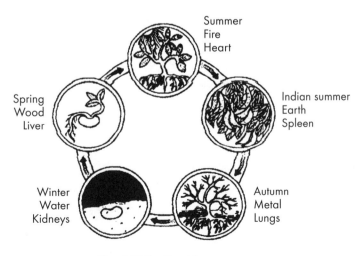

Fig. 1.7 The Five Elements

the five phases of energy is the manifestation and activity of the sun, moon, stars, planets, and all life on Earth.

This view of Taoist cosmology may seem abstract and simplistic, but modern science has arrived at essentially the same view of creation. All matter throughout the universe is made of atomic particles. The atoms, once believed to be the smallest indivisible particles of matter, have proved under observation to be made of subatomic particles and waves, all propelled into motion by the polarity of positive and negative. Scientists have also arrived at a concept of an original explosion of energy, which they refer to as the big bang.

Taoists view the universe as a vast ocean of interacting energy driven by the fundamental interplay of yin and yang. Humans are one of the most complex manifestations of such interaction.

The universe as a manifestation of the Five Elements is self-sustaining. All living creatures are constantly interacting with all the elements of creation through the processes of eating, breathing, sensing, feeling, and thinking.

FROM WHERE DO WE DERIVE OUR LIFE FORCE?

According to Taoists, the basic source of human energy comes from our parents. The yin energy of the mother in the egg and the yang energy of the father in the sperm provide the initial sparks that ignite the fire of life. This energy from the parents is called prenatal energy, or Original Chi.

A second source of chi is radiation from the stars in the form of light, electromagnetic waves, and subsonic vibrations. The most prominent stars in this process are the Sun, the North Star, and the stars in the constellation known as the Big Dipper. Humans in particular depend on the chi radiated through space by the stars and planets for sustenance. The air we breathe is charged with cosmic energy in the form of extremely fine particles of cosmic "dust." This dust is the residue of exploded stars, planets, and asteroids. It rains constantly onto the earth, forming an essential component of the soil. Plants are the only living organisms that can directly transform light into nourishment. Humans absorb light energy indirectly by eating either vegetables or the flesh of other animals that feed on plants.

The interaction of light, cosmic dust in the soil, and air, together with water, forms the basis for photosynthesis in plants. All life on earth depends on plant life, either directly or indirectly. The great majority of organisms feed directly on plants and a small minority feed on other animals that eat plants.

Chi is life, and abundant energy is abundant life. If our energy supply is low due to illness or excessive emotions, we experience low vitality and lack of

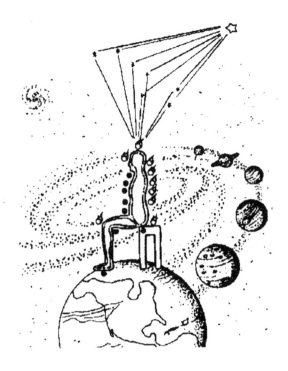

Fig. 1.8 Human connection to the universe

drive. Living ceases to be an enjoyable experience; we feel disconnected from the environment, from society, and from ourselves. Taoists therefore place extreme importance on cultivating and maintaining a high level of energy to strengthen one's connection with the universe and oneself.

The ultimate goal of Taoist practice is attaining a state of complete union with the source of the universe. All life emerges from Wu Chi unconsciously. Through Taoist practice one can attain immortality and return to the Wu Chi consciously to dissolve into oneness. Taoists actively encourage any practice or point of view that helps strengthen our connection with the universe.

The most direct way of sustaining our links with all creation is by cultivating the energy that is the foundation of all life. Tai Chi plays a central role in Taoism as one of the most efficient and effortless ways of cultivating chi and experiencing one's own energetic origins. The precise Tai Chi postures open and undo energetic blockages in one's energy channels: the slow and gentle movements stretch one's energy channels and keep them strong and supple; the rhythmic movements of the muscles, spine, and joints pump energy through the whole body. Thus Tai Chi is an exercise that gives the practitioner more energy than it uses up. After a round of Tai Chi, you feel relaxed yet invigorated.

TAI CHI: A VITAL PART OF THE UNIVERSAL TAO SYSTEM

Although Tai Chi has been practiced by laypeople for hundreds of years, it is within the overall context of Taoist practice that one can really understand Tai Chi's profound depth and importance. Historic and contemporary Taoist adepts practice Tai Chi as one part of their overall program for cultivating and developing their physical body, energy body, and spirit body. These three bodies correspond respectively to the "three treasures," or San Bao: ching or jing (sexual energy or essence), chi (the inner breath, basic life force energy), and shen (spirit or consciousness). All Taoist disciplines focus on strengthening these three aspects. No one discipline can be said to cultivate all three treasures with equal emphasis and effectiveness. For this reason, most true practitioners use an integrated combination of practices to nourish the three treasures and thus to strengthen and develop the three bodies.

As we pointed out in the introduction, in the Universal Tao system we practice a combination of sitting, standing, and moving techniques that mutually support one another and create a strong foundation for mastering the internal arts.

Microcosmic Orbit

Many people have diligently practiced Tai Chi for several years, yet they do not have a clear idea of what chi feels like. One of the requirements of advanced martial arts training is being able to sense the intention of your opponent before he or she makes a move. When a student is unable to sense his or her own energy, it is impossible to sense the energy of another person, much less the chi activating the opponent's thoughts before they manifest in action. The first step in Tai Chi Chi Kung practice, therefore, is becoming acquainted with the force that animates one's being and learning to sense, direct, and circulate it through the Microcosmic Orbit.

The Microcosmic Orbit meditation is the foundation of all the Universal Tao practices. The Microcosmic Orbit is our main energetic circuit; it feeds all the other channels in the body. Opening the Microcosmic Orbit and removing blockages along its energetic pathway releases more chi to vitalize the entire body. Through this practice the student learns to recognize what chi feels like while circulating it through the Governor meridian (running up the back) and the Functional or Conception meridian (coming down the front of the body).

When you can feel chi moving through your body, you can know whether

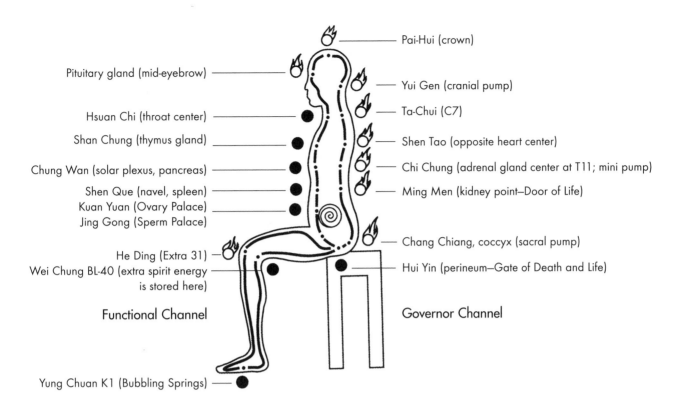

Fig. 1.9 Microcosmic Orbit

Labels, left side (Functional Channel):

Pituitary gland (mid-eyebrow)

Hsuan Chi (throat center)

Shan Chung (thymus gland)

Chung Wan (solar plexus, pancreas)

Shen Que (navel, spleen)
Kuan Yuan (Ovary Palace)
Jing Gong (Sperm Palace)

He Ding (Extra 31)
Wei Chung BL-40 (extra spirit energy is stored here)

Functional Channel

Yung Chuan K1 (Bubbling Springs)

Labels, right side (Governor Channel):

Pai-Hui (crown)

Yui Gen (cranial pump)

Ta-Chui (C7)

Shen Tao (opposite heart center)

Chi Chung (adrenal gland center at T11; mini pump)

Ming Men (kidney point—Door of Life)

Chang Chiang, coccyx (sacral pump)

Hui Yin (perineum—Gate of Death and Life)

Governor Channel

your Tai Chi posture is structurally correct by observing whether the posture opens or shuts off the energetic flow in your body. It is easier to learn the basics of chi circulation during sitting meditation, when you are not distracted by having to move and pay attention to the hundreds of other details of the Tai Chi form. Once you have become familiar with the feeling of chi circulation, you will easily begin to integrate this into your Tai Chi movements.

The Inner Smile and the Six Healing Sounds

The process of sensing one's own chi is refined in Universal Tao practice through the practices of the Inner Smile and the Six Healing Sounds.

We communicate with our organs through the Inner Smile meditation, a process of connecting with the higher self and directing a loving and appreciative awareness to the various parts of the body. We have all experienced situations in which we are total strangers in new surroundings. Sometimes when we are in a foreign country we are not even able to speak the language, yet a smile automatically communicates to others that our intention is friendly. So smiling is a form of language, a friendly language, which we use in Taoist

The Origins of Tai Chi Chi Kung

practice to communicate not only with other people but with our own vital organs and other parts of the body as well.

The Six Healing Sounds practice is a method for harmonizing and balancing the energy in the vital organs through movements, posture, and sound. Why communicate with the vital organs? In Taoist practice we recognize that the vital organs are places in the body where chi is absorbed, processed, stored, and made available for sustaining life. Becoming acquainted with the organs and sensing the chi are essential for developing sensitivity to the needs of the body and the energy that gives it life. The Six Healing Sounds practice cools and detoxifies the organs and helps us release negative emotions that begin to restrict our energy flow.

At first the Inner Smile practice may seem disconnected from the Six Healing Sounds, but later we learn to smile down to the organ we are working with at the end of each sound.

Taoists believe consciousness is rooted not in the brain alone but also in the vital organs, and, in a more subtle and refined sense, in each of the cells. The Six Healing Sounds and the Inner Smile begin the process of listening to the body and developing deep inner sensitivity. By smiling to the organs and thanking them for the work they do, eventually we reawaken the intelligence of the whole body.

In the Universal Tao, therefore, we always begin Tai Chi Chi Kung practice with the Inner Smile. This helps students relax and turn their awareness to their subtle inner sensations. Although the Six Healing Sounds are usually not directly integrated into a round of Tai Chi practice, performing them anytime during the day increases relaxation and inner awareness, and this enhanced state carries over to positively influence your Tai Chi.

Iron Shirt Chi Kung

In Universal Tao practice, energy work does not stop at sensing energy and establishing communication with the organs. Vital energy circulates within the entire structure of the physical body, so great care is taken to keep that structure in top shape.

We can have a high level of vitality, but if we constantly sit slumped, stand off-center, or walk stooped forward, eventually we create a disfiguration of the skeletal structure. In addition, the organs are unnecessarily pressured and forced to perform under internal stress. The circulation of chi then becomes blocked in places, causing energetic excesses and deficiencies that can eventually lead to illness.

To prevent or remedy damage to the physical and energetic structures, we teach a set of practices known as Iron Shirt Chi Kung. The word *kung* in Chi Kung (or in kung fu) means "intensive work." In Iron Shirt Chi Kung we work intensively with three aspects of chi: the chi in the air we breathe, the prenatal chi that has been in our bodies since conception, and the chi in the organs.

We also work with the skeletal structure, the tendons, the connective tissue that surrounds all the organs and muscles, and the bone marrow. We learn to adjust the skeletal alignment in such a way that if a great force is applied to our structure, we can redirect it to the ground so that it does not throw us off balance. By learning how to place the skeletal structure in total alignment with the force of gravity, we also facilitate the movement of vital energy in the body.

The ancient Taoists firmly believed that any change in the physical body produces a similar change in the mind and emotions. Conversely, changes in the mental and spiritual being manifest through the physical body. The integration of the structure achieved through Iron Shirt practice is eventually reflected in a more balanced energy level, better health, and greater emotional and physical stability.

The intensive work done in Iron Shirt is relatively static; the different postures are all done standing rooted to one spot. But we are not like trees that never move! Putting the principles of Iron Shirt in motion, we arrive at the practice of Tai Chi.

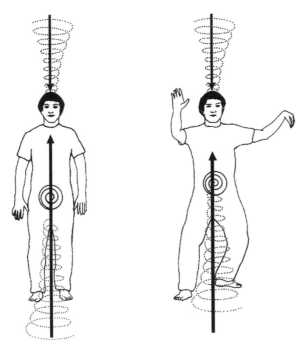

Fig. 1.10 When we know how to stand aligned with the heavenly and earthly forces, we can learn to move with them.

Healing Love through the Tao

Ching chi (or *jing chi*), the energy of our reproductive system, is the most condensed essence of energy in our bodies; just as a seed contains the entire tree, so too does our sexual energy contain the condensed essence of an entire human being.

In all life-forms that multiply sexually, a tremendous amount of energy goes into the reproductive system. If this energy does not go into creating offspring and is not recycled into the body, it is simply lost. This loss is a great drain of life force; in fact, many plants die shortly after going to seed and many animals die soon after reproducing.

Tai Chi Chi Kung practice helps lay the foundation for the Taoist inner alchemical transformation of ching into chi, chi into shen, and shen into Wu Chi. Conservation of sexual energy is a prerequisite for transformation. It is therefore essential that the Tai Chi Chi Kung practitioner learn the methods of Healing Love through the Tao for conserving sexual energy.

Healing Love also teaches practitioners how to balance the yin and yang aspects of their sexual energy. Many famous Tai Chi masters who did not know the Taoist secrets of love became too yang and sought to disperse their excess

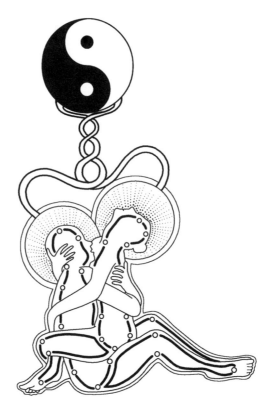

Fig. 1.11 Healing Love practice

yang in unhealthy ways, such as through sexual excess, drugs, and alcohol. Of course, many of these masters died relatively young, failing to exemplify the fruits of long life that Tai Chi practice is famous for yielding.

Bone Marrow Nei Kung

Tai Chi masters are also famous for having extraordinarily strong and dense bones, like steel wrapped in cotton. A recent experiment in China showed absolutely no evidence of osteoporosis in a group of both female and male Tai Chi practitioners over the age of eighty.

In Taoist physiology the sexual essence is stored in the kidneys, the organs that rule the reproductive system. The kidneys also rule the bones, the marrow, and the brain. The Taoist sexual energy practices keep the reproductive organs fit and healthy. When Tai Chi is combined with the practices of Healing Love, Iron Shirt, and Bone Marrow Nei Kung, the essence of sexual energy is recycled and directed to the bones to strengthen and restore both the bone matrix and the marrow.

INTEGRATING YOUR MEDITATIONS INTO MOVEMENT

Once the student has a clear sense of what chi feels like, the next step is to learn to relax sufficiently to allow chi and mind to move the structure. Once the student knows how to stand in alignment with the heavenly and earth forces, then it is not hard to learn to move in total alignment at all times. Once the student has developed a sense of rootedness to the ground, as well as mental focus and stability through meditation, then it is not hard to learn to carry in these same qualities to daily activity.

The practice of Tai Chi is thus a further refinement of the sitting practice in Microcosmic Orbit meditation and the standing practices of Iron Shirt Chi Kung; it carries the centeredness developed in meditation and Iron Shirt into the movements of daily life, giving a more complete sense of well-being.

Why Practice Tai Chi Chi Kung?

The initial attraction of Tai Chi practice lies in the beauty and grace of its movements. Unlike the Japanese and Korean forms, Tai Chi does not require strenuous effort to accomplish. It can also be practiced into quite an advanced age without danger. By contrast, some of the "hard" forms of martial arts can cause severe damage to the joints if improperly practiced and are too vigorous for most elderly people.

TAI CHI CHI KUNG IMPROVES POSTURE

One of the most important benefits of Tai Chi practice is the improvement it creates in posture. Poor posture results from a combination of negative emotional states and lack of self-awareness. We are all familiar with the picture of a chronically depressed person: stooped and weighed down at the shoulders, as if the whole world were pressing down on him or her. This posture reflects the negative emotional states of sadness, indifference, withdrawal, fear, defensiveness, and so on. Once these negative emotions become chronically established, they imprint onto the physical frame. These dysfunctional malformations then prevent the person from experiencing a harmonious and balanced emotional state.

One of the exercises we often do in workshops is to ask participants first to sit in a fully energized position, allowing that posture to evoke the feelings of courage, grounding, strength, and emotional well-being. Then we ask the participants to slowly slump down in their chairs, heads hanging down. In

Fig. 2.1 Poor posture is a combination of negative emotional scars and lack of self-awareness.

Fig. 2.2 A slumped posture prevents the life force from moving efficiently.

this slumped position they report feelings of sadness, depression, and lack of energy.

Once participants have experienced states of both high and low energy, we ask them to sit upright in a courageous, energizing posture and again try to experience sadness, depression, and lack of energy. After some time we ask them to slump down in their chairs and try to reevoke the feelings of courage, grounding, strength, and harmony. The majority of people can neither re-create a harmonious state while slumped in the chair nor feel depressed when sitting in the posture of proper alignment.

This simple experiment—which we encourage you to try—demonstrates the important relationship between posture and emotional state. If you are unconscious of how you stand and move, you usually remain unconscious of the subtle emotional states you are generating.

One reason that meditation practice is an integral support for Tai Chi is that it generates a state of self-awareness. This self-awareness is twofold, encompassing awareness both of the energy moving within the meridians and of the structure within which the energy is moving.

The very first position of Tai Chi, Wu Chi stance, initiates the process of postural awareness. Beginning at the soles of the feet, we sense to see if all the

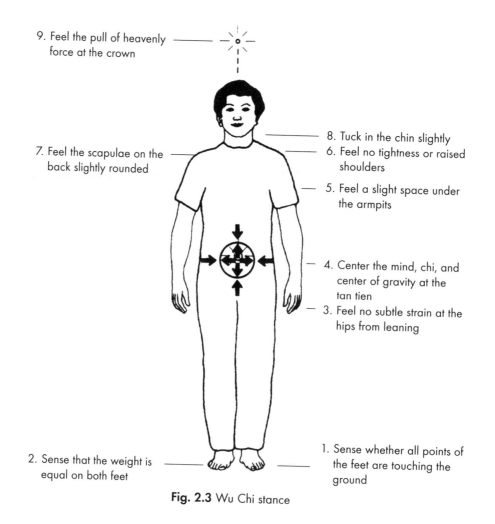

9. Feel the pull of heavenly force at the crown

8. Tuck in the chin slightly

6. Feel no tightness or raised shoulders

5. Feel a slight space under the armpits

7. Feel the scapulae on the back slightly rounded

4. Center the mind, chi, and center of gravity at the tan tien

3. Feel no subtle strain at the hips from leaning

2. Sense that the weight is equal on both feet

1. Sense whether all points of the feet are touching the ground

Fig. 2.3 Wu Chi stance

points of the feet are touching the ground. Moving upward, we sense whether one leg has more weight than the other or if there is any subtle strain at the hips from leaning in any direction. At the shoulders we sense whether there is tightness and observe if the scapulae are rounded so that the chest caves in. Reaching the head, we check the position of the chin and the base of the skull, making sure the chin is slightly tucked, allowing for a feeling of openness at the base of the skull. Finally, we align the angle of the crown until we feel a subtle upward energy pull, focusing on a ball of chi above our crown. This pull indicates that the entire structure is fully suspended between the pull of the heavenly force above and that of the earth force below.

Structural alignment is a natural function of the human body, but we tend to lose that alignment after childhood. Through Tai Chi practice we consciously and constantly readjust the posture until proper structural alignment becomes part of our natural bodily knowledge once again and we no longer slump unconsciously for long. This improvement in physical posture is immediately reflected in improved mental and emotional outlook. The self-awareness that awakens us to misaligned posture also awakens us to negative emotional states that we might not otherwise notice.

Proper posture also plays a key role in healthy energy circulation. (This is demonstrated in the exercise of sitting in the depressed and energized positions.) A person feels energized simply because the posture of courage allows the energy to flow better; similarly, people feel depressed because the slumped posture prevents the life force from moving efficiently.

Taoist practice has shown over thousands of years of experience that poor energy circulation plays a major role in illness. When we encourage proper energy circulation through meditation, exercise, and positive mental states, the incidence of illness decreases rapidly.

TAI CHI CHI KUNG STRENGTHENS THE NERVOUS SYSTEM

One of the most damaging aspects of contemporary life is the destructive effects of pollution, uncontrolled negative emotions, and urban overcrowding on a person's central nervous system. Advertisements for remedies to relieve headache, stomach upset, insomnia, constipation, and so on reflect the sad state of the modern nervous system.

The nervous system is the electrochemical mechanism through which the body regulates all of its functions. Life force, in the form of electromagnetic impulses, is the means the nervous system uses to effect communication. The improved energy circulation experienced through meditation and Tai Chi has a regenerating effect on the nervous system.

TAI CHI CHI KUNG BENEFITS CHRONIC ILLNESS STATES

Another positive aspect of meditation and Tai Chi practice is their effect on illnesses already present. While reviewing many of the English publications on Tai Chi in preparation for this book, I was impressed by the life stories of the serious practitioners. Many of the great figures of contemporary Tai Chi began their Tai Chi practice due to serious illnesses that modern medicine had deemed to be chronic or terminal.

The improvement in energy circulation and the transformation of negative emotional and mental states are significant factors in the elimination of illness. Thanks to the work of modern researchers such as Dr. Bernie Siegel and Dr. Herbert Benson, Western medicine is beginning to recognize that certain chronic and terminal illnesses that do not respond to pharmaceutical or surgical treatments can be cured through a change in the mental and emotional outlook of the patient when combined with some form of energizing exercise.

TAI CHI CHI KUNG CLEARS NEGATIVE EMOTIONS

Being able to move freely, calmly, and effortlessly is one of the natural traits of a healthy body. So is the ability to experience and express the complete range of human emotions, both positive and negative. Holding on to emotions and not releasing them fully is one of the main causes of tension and stress, creating blockages to energy flow and eventually leading to illness.

A clear and honest awareness of one's inner state is one of the results of successful meditation practice. This same awareness is expanded in Tai Chi practice, so that little by little one is able to notice in one's movement the subtle areas of tension and holding. Discovering an area of tightness and tension, the practitioner can become aware of the emotional pattern behind the "body armoring" that is causing the tension. The student can then apply a wide range of methods to help dissolve that armoring. Borrowing from the meditation practice of the Inner Smile, you can smile to these areas during Tai Chi practice and send positive feelings to dissolve tensions. The practitioner can also direct the life force to areas that need healing.

TAI CHI CHI KUNG BENEFITS THE CONNECTIVE TISSUE, TENDONS, MUSCLES, AND CIRCULATION OF CHI

The life force has a very definite physical structure through which it moves. Over the last forty years, research has been carried out in Asia and the West to determine the precise pathways of the life force. Recent studies have focused on the role of the connective tissue in energy transmission.

The connective tissue, or fascia, is a very thin layer of tissue that pervades the whole organism, enveloping the organs, muscles, tissues, and bones. As its name implies, the connective tissue connects. The most visible aspect of the connective tissue is the fascia, but at the microscopic level, connective tissues extend into every cell in the body, linking each cell with the rest of the organism.

In terms of its relevance to Tai Chi, the most important research on the connective tissue has focused on its bioelectrical and biochemical properties.

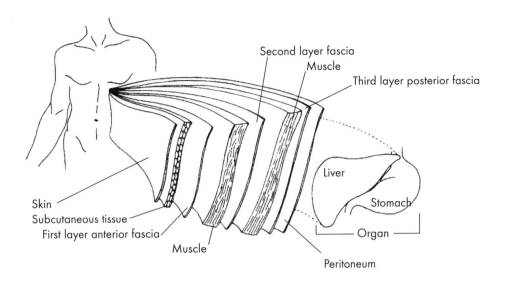

Fig. 2.4 The fascial layers

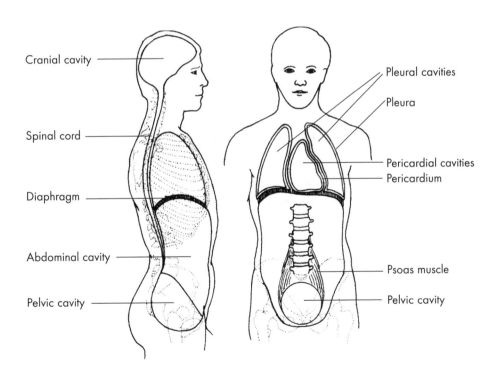

Fig. 2.5 Each organ has a fascial layer covering its cavity.

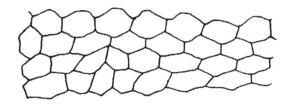

Fig. 2.6a Connective tissue has a lattice structure.

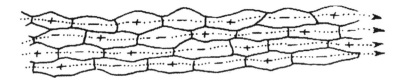

Fig. 2.6b When exercising, the lattice structure compresses, generating bioelectrical signals.

It has been discovered that the connective tissue functions as a vast electrical communication system, linking every single cell of the body with every other.

When viewed through a microscope, the connective tissue looks like a complex crystalline lattice structure. When we perform simple movements the crystalline lattice structure is compressed, generating bioelectrical signals. It is now suspected that the traditional meridian system of Chinese medicine may be closely linked with the pervasive connective tissue.

In the vast repertoire of Taoist exercises no practices can be found for developing bulky musculature, as in Western bodybuilding. The main reason is the Taoist focus on tendon power. Muscles are developed through heavy physical exercise, but even if a person weight-trains every day for the rest of his or her life, there is an age at which the muscles begin to decline in strength and size. The muscle tissue breaks down and is no longer rebuilt as efficiently as it is in youth. Muscle tissue also demands many of the nutrients we take in to nourish and maintain itself.

The tendons, by contrast, are not affected by age and require very little vascularization for maintenance. If a person has developed strong tendons through an exercise regimen, then that tendon power can be maintained until a ripe old age. The tendons act like thick rubber bands that naturally contract. Together with the muscles, the tendons facilitate the movement of the bone structure.

The practice of Iron Shirt Chi Kung introduces different methods for strengthening the tendons. One of the goals of Iron Shirt is to relax the muscles as much as possible, engaging the tendons to hold the structure while standing. This training carries over into Tai Chi practice.

The advantage of developing tendon power is that the musculature can then be more relaxed in movement. With this muscular relaxation, the connective tissue is able to transport electrical impulses and life force much more efficiently. In Tai Chi one learns how to move in a state of muscular relaxation, allowing the tendons and the life force in the connective tissue to provide "inner" strength.

Basic Principles of Tai Chi Chi Kung

Tai Chi Chi Kung is grounded in the principles of the Tao. The extent to which you have incorporated and integrated these principles into your movements determines your level of mastery. It does not matter if you know a long or a short Tai Chi form; what counts is knowledge and application of the Tai Chi principles.

This chapter introduces the basic principles of Tai Chi Chi Kung. Study them, memorize them, and apply them in your movements. The best way to practice initially is to take one principle at a time and work on it until you can do it automatically, without conscious thought. Then work on the next principles in the same way until you have mastered them all.

The second half of this book introduces the more advanced Tai Chi Chi Kung principles. Do not worry about learning these until you have mastered the more basic principles included in this chapter and have gained competence in the Tai Chi Chi Kung form (or another Tai Chi style) as presented in chapter 5.

Eventually, with daily practice, you will discover that you have incorporated the Tai Chi principles into your everyday life—as you sit, walk, stand, and lie down, you will notice that you are moving in a fresh, effortless, and beautiful way. This is the reward of Tai Chi Chi Kung.

Here, then, are the basic principles of Tai Chi Chi Kung.

STAY ROOTED IN EACH MOVEMENT

In Tai Chi Chi Kung, rooting means being connected with the ground. All forms of energy work require that the practitioner remain solidly rooted. Unfortunately, rooting is poorly understood outside of martial arts circles. Many longtime practitioners of meditation have never even heard of rooting. Imagine an electrician who has never heard about grounding the line! He is bound for disaster sooner or later.

Tai Chi practice integrates physical rooting into the very way a person moves through life. The practice of psychic rooting is cultivated through meditation. Physical and energetic rooting is developed through Iron Shirt and Tai Chi, as a support to the mental and emotional changes that take place via meditation. One reflects the other. The grounding cultivated through Tai Chi manifests as stability in movements. Emotionally, it manifests as a stable personality with clarity of purpose and full command of the willpower. As an aspect of spiritual cultivation in the Tao, rooting is very important; Tai Chi and Iron Shirt practice develop this ability.

Tai Chi is also a martial art, and its emphasis on rooting is one of the facets that has made Tai Chi a superior system of self-defense. In Tai Chi, power and

Fig. 3.1 All forms of energy work require that we remain solidly connected to the ground.

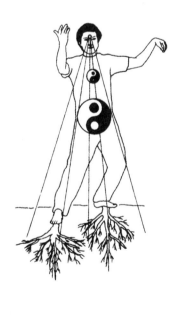

Fig. 3.2 In Tai Chi, rooting means more than just standing on the ground. Rooting begins with the mental, emotional, and spiritual aspects of the personality.

stability come from structural alignment with the ground. A person becomes very hard to knock over when he or she is aligned; opponents may feel as though they have just run into a solid tree with deep roots. When aligned, practitioners attack with the support of the earth behind their movements. This aligned force is then directed, with all the parts of the skeletal framework working together with integrity.

By contrast, many martial artists train specific parts of the body in isolation. They work to develop strong arm and leg muscles in particular, and when they punch, they are using mainly the strength of the arm and shoulder. How can one part of the body acting alone be as powerful as the united and integrated strength of the whole body? Other martial arts styles may use the force of the waist and legs in punches, but practitioners who are not rooted and do not have correct structural alignment still lack true power.

MAINTAIN YOUR CENTER OF GRAVITY IN THE LOWER TAN TIEN

In Tai Chi we seek to maintain perfect balance and stability throughout all of our movements, both in solo practice of the Tai Chi form and in Tai Chi martial arts applications. For optimum stability, in Tai Chi one trains to keep the center of gravity low in the body, in the area between the navel, the Door of Life (the lumbar spine), and the sexual center—the approximate midpoint of the body. This area is known as the lower tan tien. Keeping the center of gravity in the lower tan tien is relatively easy in sitting. The moment a person stands up and begins to move, however, the center of gravity adjusts itself to the particular movement.

A baby's first attempt at moving around in the world is by crawling. A baby crawling on the floor has a low center of gravity. Later, as its leg bones began to solidify, the baby attempts to stand up. For a few weeks the baby goes through the process of standing and falling until she or he learns the trick of raising the center of gravity and staying centered. From there, the child gradually accomplishes the more difficult feats of walking, trotting, running, bicycle riding, and sports, where balance is refined to a higher degree.

As a person grows older, the center of gravity rises to a fluctuating point in the torso. As the person experiences negative emotions, the center of gravity begins to travel farther upward in the torso. When a person becomes angry, the center of gravity can rise up to the chest, causing enough energetic pressure to produce a heart attack. In extreme fright, the center of gravity may rise

1. Center of gravity is very low
2. Center of gravity slightly higher
3. Center balanced between navel and legs
4. Center balanced between abdomen and sloar plexus
5. Center very high, between upper head and chest

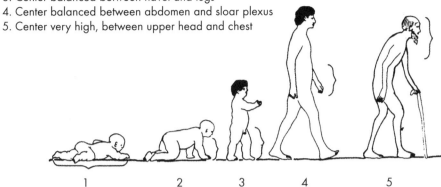

1   2   3   4   5

Fig. 3.4 The center of gravity changes with age.

all the way to the throat, making the person unable to utter a sound.

By the time a man or woman reaches adulthood, the center of gravity may be permanently based somewhere in the upper chest, making the person top heavy. That is why elderly people tend to fall easily and often need the assistance of walking sticks.

The process of relearning to become centered is easier at first while sitting or standing in one place. Movement adds another dimension to the learning experience. In the Universal Tao system, therefore, the Microcosmic Orbit meditation and Iron Shirt practices are taught before Tai Chi.

In the Microcosmic Orbit meditation, the practitioner begins by learning to focus the awareness at the area of the lower tan tien, the midpoint of the

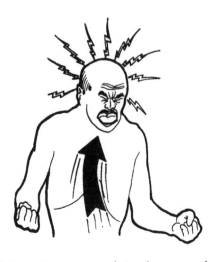

Fig. 3.5 Excessive anger can bring the center of gravity
high up in the chest or the throat.

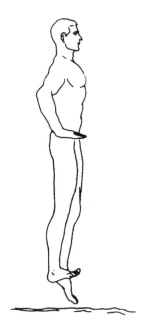

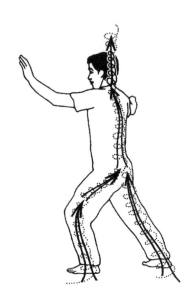

Fig. 3.6 A person with a high center of gravity lives disconnected from the earth.

Fig. 3.7 In Tai Chi we keep the center of gravity low, maintaining a strong connection with the ground. This is rooting.

body. As the breath becomes even and the body relaxes, the center of gravity naturally drops down to the navel area. In Iron Shirt Chi Kung, a similar process takes place. The person stands in any of five positions; by exhaling, relaxing the chest and diaphragm, and controlling the breath at the lower abdomen, the center of gravity shifts down to the lower tan tien.

The next stage in working with the center of gravity is to move the structure while keeping the center low at all times. This sounds simple, but it takes practice. In Tai Chi we keep the center of gravity low by learning to move in alignment with the heavenly and earthly forces, generating our movements from the hips and remaining mentally and physically connected to the ground.

Centeredness and grounding are brought about not only by mechanical knowledge of the physical structure but also by corresponding emotional and mental states. If one is able to experience emotions and then let go and relax, the center of gravity returns to a place somewhere in the lower torso and all is well. However, if a person never lets go of emotions and tends to dwell in the past, that person will lack presence. The body will be characterized by a high center of gravity.

Through meditation practice, the student learns to keep the mind centered at the lower tan tien. The tan tien energy, guided by the mind, directs all movements. In Tai Chi, this practice is developed further; Tai Chi practice uses the mental power developed through meditation to direct the life force to any bodily point. If the practitioner wants to turn left, for example, the mind directs the tan tien chi to turn left and the energy guides the hips into the turn. The same applies to moving forward and to sinking back.

KEEP THE BODY VERTICALLY ALIGNED, AS IF SUSPENDED FROM THE CROWN

Another Tai Chi principle is to keep your body aligned with gravity, awakening the thrusting channels that penetrate through the body's core as a central axis around which you can pivot freely and easily. This is also described as feeling the head as if it is suspended from a string attached to a chi ball or a star above.

In a misdirected effort to keep the spine erect, many people struggle to stretch the head up from below. Instead, train yourself to guide the chi flow into the spine. This stretches and lifts the spine effortlessly upward. Awareness of chi at the crown (the Bai Hui point, Governing Vessel 20) calms and relaxes you while aligning your body with the heavenly force.

Gravity acts on the physical structure by exerting a vertical pull in relation to the ground. This vertical pull aligns from the crown through the perineum to the soles of the feet. In Tai Chi movements, the practitioner maintains this

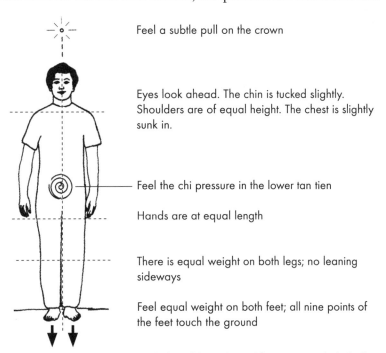

Feel a subtle pull on the crown

Eyes look ahead. The chin is tucked slightly. Shoulders are of equal height. The chest is slightly sunk in.

Feel the chi pressure in the lower tan tien

Hands are at equal length

There is equal weight on both legs; no leaning sideways

Feel equal weight on both feet; all nine points of the feet touch the ground

Fig. 3.8 Standing fully erect, feeling suspended as if by a thread from a star or chi ball, the energy flows up, energizing the organs and generating a feeling of well-being.

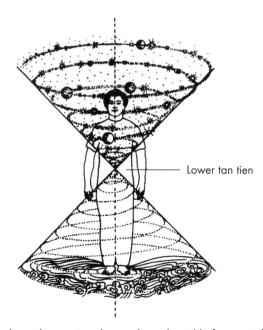

Fig. 3.9 Perfect balance harmonizes heavenly and earthly forces at the tan tien.

Lower tan tien

central line of gravity, whether moving forward, sinking back, or turning. All movements emanate from the center, both physically and mentally.

The human structure is like a tree. The feet are the roots, the torso and legs are the trunk, and the arms are the branches. The inner foundation of Tai Chi is the life force; the outer foundation is the feet. The feet support the body's entire weight and at the same time they connect with the earth force. In Taoism the feet are considered the ground wire of the body.

A chair or table is most stable when its weight is supported equally by all four legs. Similarly, a person is most stable when the weight is evenly divided

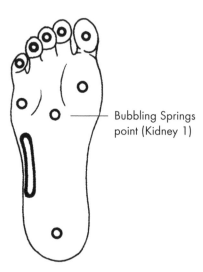

Bubbling Springs point (Kidney 1)

Fig. 3.10 K1 and the nine points of the foot

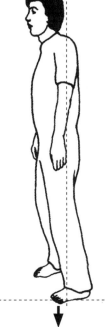

Fig. 3.11 Leaning forward changes the path of the central line of gravity.

over the nine points of the foot. These nine points are the heel, the outer edge, the small ball, the large ball, and each of the five toes. In Tai Chi we take great care to place these nine points evenly in contact with the ground each time we step and shift weight; thus the weight is poised over the middle of the foot, a point known as Bubbling Springs. This point is so named because when we align the body's weight over it, the earth energy seems to freely flow up into the body, just like a bubbling geyser.

When a person stands straight, with the central line of gravity perfectly aligned from the crown through the perineum and down to the feet, the weight is equally distributed over the nine points of the feet. This is called Perfect Balance of the Heaven.

When a person leans one way or another, the central line of gravity no longer runs from the crown down through the perineum. The line of gravity changes according to whichever way one is leaning, and it is no longer equally distributed over the nine points of the feet. For example, when the body leans forward just a little, there is more weight on the balls of the feet and less on the heels. The center of gravity, according to one's height, weight, and flexibility, is somewhere up in the chest. A person who is shoved or pulled while in this position will fall forward easily.

Many people have the habit of leaning forward when walking. People who walk leaning forward with a high center of gravity are actually falling; what

Basic Principles
of Tai Chi
Chi Kung

35

prevents them from falling down is the rapid movement of their legs. Excess tension is the result of this posture, and that drains energy. Through habit these people may become numb to what is actually happening, but the nervous system knows better—the person experiences deep tiredness and fatigue because of this uneconomical use of energy.

The habit of leaning has destructive effects on both the physical body and energy circulation. Leaning causes compression in certain organs, affecting their energy flow. Leaning also disturbs the pumping action of the diaphragm, making the heart work harder in order to pump the blood. Any interference with the diaphragm affects the breath and, ultimately, the mind. Energy blockages created through leaning eventually distort the physical structure, the powers of the mind, and the emotions.

Hip and spinal cord problems often result from not evenly distributing the body's weight over the nine points of the feet. People can observe from the way the soles of their shoes wear out how evenly they stand and walk on the feet.

There are certain Tai Chi styles, notably Wu style, in which practitioners appear to lean forward when pushing. Yet, when we analyze the practitioners' structures we find that the spine remains straight and perpendicular to the hip bone, exactly as if they were standing straight. What appears to be a high center of gravity is counterbalanced by the extension of the rear leg, so the center of gravity remains in the lower tan tien. The overall structure is like a stick, leaning at an angle yet firmly connected to the ground. The "leaning" stance in these tai chi styles is just as effective as the vertical stances used in the Tai Chi Chi Kung form.

BREATHE WITH THE LOWER ABDOMEN

When a newborn emerges from the womb, the first thing the infant does is take a deep breath. We can survive without food for weeks, we can live without water for several days, but we cannot do without oxygen for more than a few minutes.

Breathing is both a voluntary and an involuntary function of the body. We can consciously change the way we breathe and even stop breathing at will, but we cannot voluntarily hold the breath to the point of suffocation; there is an automatic mechanism in the body that prevents us from doing so. Breathing and brain function are intimately connected. In accident cases in which the victim has stopped breathing, the most immediate danger to the organism is brain damage.

Ancient Taoists discovered that the breath is connected not only with

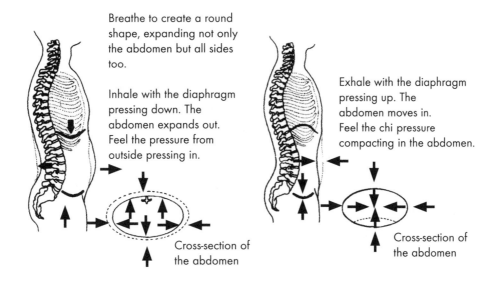

Breathe to create a round shape, expanding not only the abdomen but all sides too.

Inhale with the diaphragm pressing down. The abdomen expands out. Feel the pressure from outside pressing in.

Exhale with the diaphragm pressing up. The abdomen moves in. Feel the chi pressure compacting in the abdomen.

Cross-section of the abdomen

Cross-section of the abdomen

Fig. 3.12 Abdominal breathing

the brain but also with consciousness itself. Taoist meditators of the past left a tremendous written legacy in more than a thousand volumes, collectively known as the Taoist Canon. Many of these texts focus on the importance of breathing and present numerous breathing methods for health and spiritual development. This extensive repertoire of breathing exercises makes Taoism one of the world's most comprehensive yogas.

When the breath is calm, even, and steady, the mind experiences these same qualities. Conversely, when the breath is labored, rough, or uneven, the mind is affected by all manner of wavering feelings and emotions. The next time you see a person get very angry, notice his or her breathing pattern. Numerous modern therapies recommend deep, even, rhythmic breathing exercises as a means for restoring calmness to emotionally disturbed patients.

Tai Chi practice is always done in conjunction with abdominal breathing. Abdominal breathing simply involves keeping the abdomen relaxed while breathing. During inhalation the diaphragm moves down and during exhalation it moves up. When the lower abdominal muscles are relaxed during inhalation the abdomen can expand, there is more room for the diaphragm to move down, and more air is taken into the lungs. We breathe more fully and are therefore more energized.

When the abdomen is constricted by muscular tension, the diaphragm cannot expand fully. We automatically compensate by expanding the chest; this is called shallow chest breathing. Chest breathing is less energizing because the lungs cannot expand as much as during abdominal breathing.

Basic Principles of Tai Chi Chi Kung

Physiologically, the intercostal muscles of the chest are designed to provide only about 25 percent of the muscular force necessary to fill the lungs. The remaining 75 percent of effort is the diaphragm's job.

Lower abdominal breathing helps keep the center of gravity low. It is associated with calmness and relaxation. High-chest breathing and keeping a high center of gravity are neurologically associated with stress, anxiety, and hypertension. One recent research study revealed that over 70 percent of hypertensive patients were high-chest breathers. In a British study, over 90 percent of agoraphobic patients (people with an irrational fear of leaving the house) were successfully treated simply by teaching them to shift the breath into the lower abdomen when phobic symptoms began to occur. The next time you see someone get upset, observe whether he or she is breathing with the lower abdomen or whether the chest is heaving. Emotional balance is easily restored by the calming effect that abdominal breathing has on the mind.

Lower abdominal breathing also benefits blood circulation. The heart is the main organ responsible for pumping blood throughout the body. The up-and-down movement of the diaphragm increases and decreases the pressure in the lower abdominal cavity, home to the aorta and vena cava. This creates a pumping action that effectively reduces the heart's workload by assisting the venous blood to return to the heart. In this way, the lower abdomen serves as a second heart.

Constipation caused by abdominal tension can often be relieved by the gentle massaging action of abdominal breathing as well.

Abdominal breathing is easier when the body relearns to keep the spine aligned with the earthly and heavenly forces. When the spine is always bent forward, the diaphragm cannot move freely during respiration.

Lower abdominal breathing is the natural way to breathe; every healthy baby is born knowing how to do it. As we get older and experience the stresses and traumas of life, we become hardened physically, emotionally, and mentally. Little by little the muscles of the abdomen and the diaphragm become tight in some places and flabby in others, and we lose most of our inherent ability to breathe deeply.

Relearning abdominal breathing requires two things: first, we must loosen up emotionally; and second, we must strengthen the abdominal muscles that have become weak from lack of use.

The most effective way of cultivating even, deep breathing is through the practice known as bottle breathing. Bottle breathing is named for the way liquid fills an empty bottle. When liquid is poured into a bottle, the liquid fills the bottle from the bottom up. Deep breathing is exactly the same. The nose

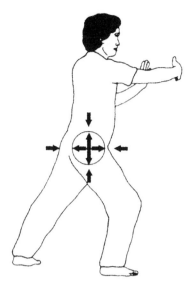

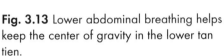

Fig. 3.13 Lower abdominal breathing helps keep the center of gravity in the lower tan tien.

Fig. 3.14 In bottle breathing the lowest part of the "bottle," the lower abdomen, fills up first.

is the opening and the lower abdomen is the bottom of the bottle. In bottle breathing we learn to inhale gently and steadily, relaxing the muscles of the lower abdomen. As the air penetrates and expands the lungs, the diaphragm expands downward. If the muscles of the abdomen are relaxed, then the diaphragm's downward expansion makes the lower abdomen expand.

To learn abdominal breathing you can do a very simple exercise in bed just before sleeping. Simply lie on your back, legs and arms extended and relaxed. Your clothes should be wide and loose, especially at the waist. Place a heavy book or brick on your lower abdomen. Inhale slowly and as deeply as possible, then exhale slowly and steadily through parted lips until all the air is exhaled. Close the mouth and begin to inhale through the nose slowly but steadily, watching the book rise as the abdomen expands. You might place your head on a pillow to more easily see the book rise and fall with the breath.

This simple exercise of abdominal weight lifting allows the body to become reacquainted with the lower abdominal muscles. With regular practice, this exercise greatly strengthens the abdomen. During Iron Shirt Chi Kung practice, we regularly combine lower abdominal breathing with packing breath, inhaling into the lower abdomen while pulling up on the anal muscles and gently pressing down with the diaphragm.

In Tai Chi, it is not necessary to practice the packing breath per se, but we still combine lower abdominal breathing with a subtle tightening of the anal

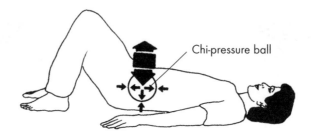

Chi-pressure ball

Fig. 3.15 Learn to build up the chi pressure

muscles. We call this "sealing the bottom"; it prevents the energy from leaking out through flaccid anal muscles.

Maintaining a firm but gentle chi pressure in the lower abdomen is the heart of developing the chi for Tai Chi practice. When you inhale, feel the lower abdomen inflating and expanding to form a chi-pressure ball in the lower tan tien; simultaneously feel a corresponding pressure pushing in from outside. As you exhale, lightly press the chi ball down with your diaphragm and abdominal muscles. You should feel the inside pressure pressing out and at the same time feel the outer pressure pressing in.

Gradually you will feel an internal chi ball building up inside. Once you do, you can start to spiral the chi ball and slowly move the chi ball down to the coccyx and up the spine, up to the crown of the head, down to the tongue and down the front of your body to the navel, and back to the tan tien. Soon you can guide the chi to the arms and legs.

Because the series of Tai Chi movements is performed slowly, it is possible to learn to regulate the breath and calm the mind. The regulation of breath begins by learning how to breathe with the abdomen, but eventually, as the body opens up and the energy begins flowing, Tai Chi practitioners feel as though they are breathing with the whole body.

Meditation practice is one of the best methods for learning to regulate the breath. Once a student has learned to regulate the breath through sitting or standing meditation, he or she learns to sustain regulated breath in movement through Tai Chi practice; hence, Tai Chi is often called moving meditation. The proper structure within each movement allows the breath to permeate the whole organism.

Breathing low down into the abdominal region, breathing through the skin, and breathing into the bone marrow are learned in Iron Shirt Chi Kung. In Tai Chi we combine these breathing techniques with relaxation and energy circulation and then put it all into motion.

OPEN THE JOINTS THROUGH GENTLE INWARD ROTATION

Another important aspect of Tai Chi is opening all the joints in the body. The stresses of modern life often first affect the joints (arthritis) and particularly the spinal vertebrae (back problems). Stress on the spinal cord obstructs the flow of chi. These obstructions further affect the organs, glands, and immune system, eventually leading to illness.

Taoists regard the joints as energy gates or centers where chi can be stored and generated. The tendons are linked to these centers. All the Tai Chi movements develop these centers by opening the joints and strengthening the tendons so the chi and tendon force can be stored and released at will.

The early Taoists found that, with Tai Chi practice, small internal movements generate joint-stored chi and its associated tendon force, while big external movements generate muscle force. Through the practices of internal development, when the joints are filled to capacity with chi, the chi begins to fill the bones. The inner rotation of the joints and tendons must be performed slowly, using the mind to guide the chi to the joints and tendons. The joints will open and act like a cushion. Then the chi can be absorbed into the bones. With fast movement, there is no time for the mind to guide and direct chi absorption. This parallels the way of nature: the strongest trees are not the ones that shoot up quickly; the strongest trees grow slowly over hundreds of years.

The hip joint is the first joint we train to open. This joint is part of the *kua*, which also includes the psoas muscles and the soft tissue, vessels, and meridians of the inguinal (groin) region. When the hip joint is closed, the groin becomes blocked and the blood vessels, lymph, and nerves in the area fold and close. This causes circulation problems and stops the chi from flowing freely. To practice opening the groin and hip joints, keep the knees loose and open but not bent too much. Learn to sink down from the hip joints and feel the weight drop directly from the pelvis to the heels, not to the knees. To further help the hip joints open, concentrate on the ankle joints; direct the chi from the hip joints into the ankle joints and then into the big toes.

The spinal joints are the second set of joints that we focus on opening. To open the spinal joints you can practice building the chi in the lower tan tien (the abdomen), feeling the chi ball and the chi pressure there. Use the mind to spiral the chi in the abdomen, as if rolling a ball from front to back, and let the energy build up. Then guide the chi into the coccyx and up the spine, pushing the energy into the spaces between the discs that separate the vertebrae. This will elongate the spine. You can also use meditation to help feel the chi open the spine. Feel a string through the center of the spine pulling the crown of the head upward. Imagine that the string is connected with a star overhead; feel this string lift the body and elongate the spine. Once the spine opens, the energy will flow to the second thoracic vertebra (T2) and the seventh cervical vertebra (C7) and down to the arms and hands.

To help open all of the joints in the body, grow the chi in the joints of the index fingers and the big toes.

INTEGRATE THE ENTIRE STRUCTURE AND SPIRAL THE EARTH FORCE

The earth force begins to travel up the legs when we are able to do three things simultaneously. First, we relax the feet to connect with the earth force. Second, we spiral a foot outward to create a screwing motion upward. And third, we push upward, as if preparing to jump.

Once the earth force spirals up to the hip, we allow it to continue up the spine by turning the hips to fully face the object of discharge. This hip motion allows the rising earth force to continue spiraling up the spine to the C7 vertebra, the juncture of the arm and neck. We then allow the earth force to continue spiraling out of the discharging arm by sinking the chest and moving the chin slightly back, as if recoiling from a push. This combination of movements takes place in an instant.

All these seemingly separate actions of spiraling and discharge work only if all the movements are actually coordinated as one motion, so we must become quite skillful at moving in one piece.

The ability to spiral the earth force properly is not a purely mechanical skill. As in all aspects of Tai Chi, the mind plays a central role. Without the ability to focus the mind on a single point, the force one is trying to discharge becomes dissipated by varying degrees. The practitioner should integrate the mind, body, and spirit into one. Opening the Belt Channels through the Fusion of the Five Elements meditation greatly enhances one's ability to spiral the chi around and through the body. Several aspects of this internal spiraling movement will be covered in later chapters in this book.

GENTLY TWIST THE ANKLE JOINTS

The ankle joints are the place where one begins the process of transferring the body force and chi to the ground and from the ground to the torso and arms. Pressing through the soles of the feet and gently twisting the ankle joints helps transfer the weight into the ground. Similar to the way a propeller converts fluid force into motion, this rotation converts body force to earth force, which can then travel up the legs to the spine, adding to one's internal structural strength.

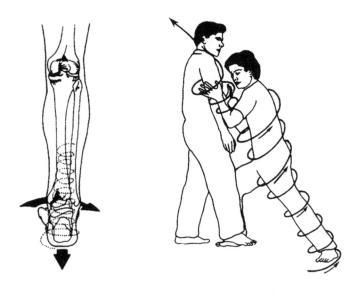

Fig. 3.16 Twisting the ankle joint very slightly outward while pressing the foot to the earth helps transfer the earth force up.

GENTLY SPIRAL THE KNEE JOINTS

The spiraling action that begins with the ankle joints now connects to the knee joints, the next vital phase in transferring the earth force from the ground to the hip. This is done by placing the feet firmly on the ground and lightly twisting the femurs outward, bringing a slight twist at the knees. This action twists and crosses the tibias and fibulas, the two bones of the lower legs, creating an extremely strong force. Tests have shown that when the Tai Chi practitioner twists in this way, the bones can withstand up to two thousand pounds (one ton) of force.

When this knee twisting is performed properly, all the tendons are rotationally wrapped around the bone, creating a strong spring force. In this position the earth, knees, and hips are in one line of power. Instead of the knees

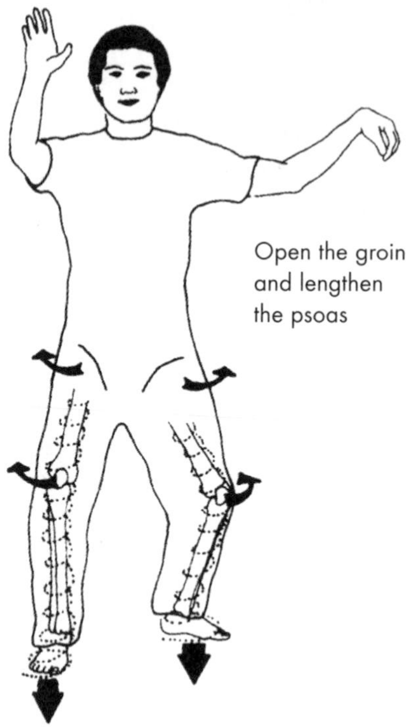

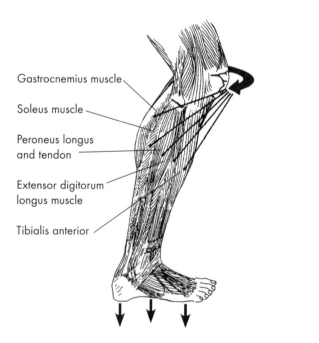

Fig. 3.17 To transfer earth forces from the ground up, twist the knee joints slightly outward.

Open the groin and lengthen the psoas

Gastrocnemius muscle

Soleus muscle

Peroneus longus and tendon

Extensor digitorum longus muscle

Tibialis anterior

Fig. 3.18 Muscles on the outside and back of the leg are activated through the feet pressing firmly against the ground and the knees spiraling outward.

Fig. 3.19 When a knee is twisted outward, all the tendons wrap around the bone, directing the energy flow upward.

Fig. 3.20 When the knee is overtwisted, the force puts a great deal of stress on it.

supporting the full weight of the body, the weight is transferred to the ankles and then to the heels and soles through to the ground. The rebounding force that springs up from the earth passes through the knees and does not jam there.

With all this twisting, it is important to reemphasize the lightness and gentleness of the desired motion. The knee is a delicate joint, and you should not overtwist it. Listen to your body: if you feel joint pain, stop! To perform Tai Chi properly, you must not use great force; rather, you slowly grow the force inwardly. Eventually you will use mainly your Yi, your mind-eye-heart power, and all the forces will move in combination spontaneously.

OPEN THE KUA AND ALIGN THE HIPS AND SACRUM

The positions of the hip joint and sacrum are very important in Tai Chi. One begins by opening the groin, or *kai kua* in Chinese; *kai kua* translates loosely as "extending the base to become firmer and stronger." The significance of the groin in producing power through all the pushing motions of Tai Chi cannot be overemphasized. When the knees are gently twisted as described above, the hip joints are opened outward and the tendons in the

Basic Principles of Tai Chi Chi Kung

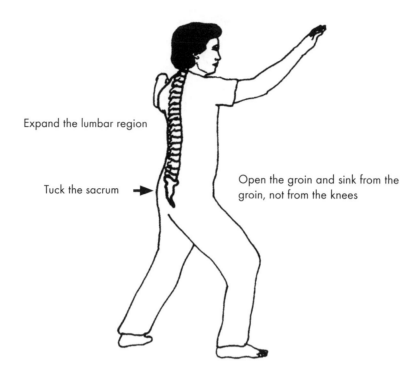

Expand the lumbar region

Tuck the sacrum ➡

Open the groin and sink from the groin, not from the knees

Fig. 3.21 When you tuck the sacrum and press the feet into the ground, the spine becomes totally aligned.

groin area become firm. This allows the transfer of force from the legs into the trunk.

The sacral alignment determines whether your structure is strong or weak. By relaxing the lower back and slightly dropping the pelvis and sacrum, as if you were tucking the tailbone between the legs, you structurally align the sacrum with the spine. When you feel the feet press more firmly into the ground, you have also aligned the sacrum with the legs; at that point you feel a line of power from the feet through the groin, to the sacrum, and up the spine. The sacrum is one of the major pumps for cerebrospinal fluid, which cushions the many nerves housed within the spine. The sacrum also helps pump the chi up the spine. Activating the sacrum by tilting and releasing it thus enhances the activities of the central nervous system.

Successfully opening the kua depends in no small measure upon the relaxing of the psoas muscles. Tai Chi Chi Kung, Iron Shirt Chi Kung, and Tao Yin are internal exercise systems that attempt to lengthen and free up the functioning of these muscles. Awareness of the psoas muscles in Tai Chi Chi Kung is vitally important. The mechanical power of Tai Chi comes from using

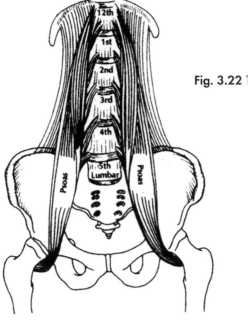

Fig. 3.22 The psoas muscles

the integrated strength of the whole body. Because the psoas muscles connect from the lower vertebrae to the lower kua (the inguinal and hip joint region), they are a major key in linking the power of the legs to the spinal column.

The psoas muscles are also closely connected to the latissimus dorsi muscles, the muscles that extend from the mid-spine to the humerus and the bones of the shoulder girdle. The psoas muscles are thus an important bridge between the lower and upper body. When the psoas muscles are relaxed and supple, the power of the legs can flow unimpeded, like a wave, from the legs to the spine and then out through the arms.

ACTIVATE THE CHI BELT AT THE WAIST

The lower tan tien, also known as the Ocean of Chi, is in the lower abdominal area; this tan tien stores and activates the Original Chi. When it is developed, the chi expands out to the kidneys, liver, spleen, small and large intestines, and sexual center. This internal expansion expresses itself outwardly, forming a chi belt like a sash around the waist.

The chi belt acts as a major bridge linking the lower part of the trunk to the upper part. If the chi belt is not developed properly, the feet, legs, and hips have no connection to the upper body. They are like soldiers without a general: they have no control and, ultimately, no power.

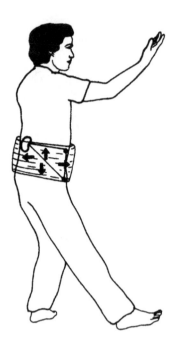

Fig. 3.23 When activating the chi belt, feel equal pressure from both inside and out.

The word *chi* in the context of the chi belt refers to the combination of breath and energy. Through Iron Shirt Chi Kung we learn to use the diaphragm to increase the lower abdominal pressure all the way around the waist. The increased pressure is similar to the role of air in a tire or that of mortar between bricks. The pressure helps fill in any weak spaces in our structure and tie the upper and lower bodies together. But the force is not static and unconscious; it is dynamic, lively, and aware, able to move with the changing movements of Tai Chi. This dynamic quality is the energy component of the chi belt.

The psoas muscles are next to the kidneys and the Door of Life point in the lumbar spine. The Door of Life is the back door to the tan tien, where our Original Chi is stored. When the psoas muscles are relaxed, the Original Chi can easily flow out into the channels and energize our movements. Furthermore, the Taoist Canon states that the connection between the kidneys (water element) and the heart (fire element) is the foundation of yin and yang balance in the body. The kidneys are like the roots, the spine is like the stem, and the heart is like the flower. The water aspect of the kidneys cools the heart while the fire aspect of the heart warms the kidneys. When the psoas muscles are loose and supple, the energy flows freely among the kidneys, spine, and heart.

The psoas muscles are also closely connected to the diaphragm. When the psoas muscles are supple, you can breathe more deeply and easily. You can fully use the power of the diaphragm and breath to support your movements and to help link the lower and upper bodies through the chi belt.

DIRECT FORCE THROUGH THE SPINAL COLUMN: POWER TRAIN

The spinal column is formed from twenty-four vertebral bones plus the sacrum and coccyx. It connects the head, arms, and legs. For chi to pass back and forth between the head and limbs, it must go through the spinal column. Alignment of the spine is thus an essential part of Tai Chi practice.

The spine, when properly aligned, is full of power and can greatly amplify the force from the legs to the arms or from the arms to the feet. By slightly tilting the sacrum and rounding the T11, T5, and C7 vertebrae, one draws the spine like a bow about to shoot an arrow.

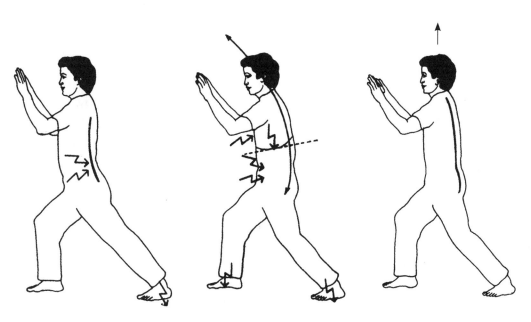

Fig. 3.24 Spinal misalignment with excessive arching of the back

Fig. 3.25 Spinal misalignment with constricted abdomen

Fig. 3.26 When the spine is aligned with gravity and just slightly bent outward, you will feel all the joints open.

SINK THE CHEST AND SHOULDERS AND ROUND THE SCAPULAE

The arms are connected to the trunk via the clavicles in the front and the scapulae in the back. The point of contact between the arm and the shoulder is at the joint of the scapula and the humerus bone. Several groups of muscles,

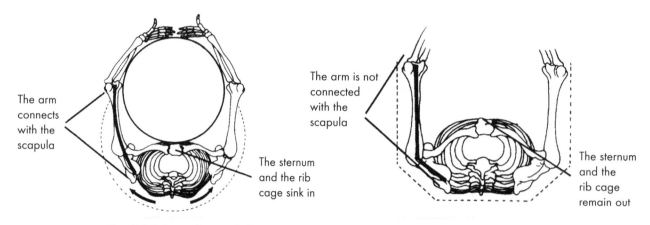

Fig. 3.27 Correctly rounded scapulae

The arm connects with the scapula

The sternum and the rib cage sink in

The arm is not connected with the scapula

The sternum and the rib cage remain out

Fig. 3.28 Incorrect rounding of the scapulae

tendons, ligaments, and connective tissues keep the bones in place and allow free movement.

The scapulae connect with the back in a structurally aligned way when you stretch the scapulae forward and sink the sternum and shoulders at the same time. In Iron Shirt Chi Kung practice, the position called Embracing the Tree is particularly useful in learning to round the scapulae and sink the shoulders and chest. See full instructions for Embracing the Tree on page 229.

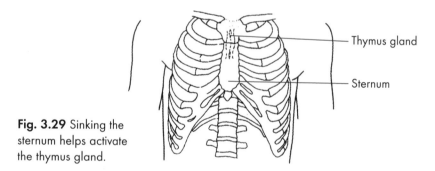

Thymus gland

Sternum

Fig. 3.29 Sinking the sternum helps activate the thymus gland.

Sinking the chest is done by exhaling a little, relaxing the chest muscles, and allowing the sternum to sink. As the sternum sinks, there is a corresponding movement of the scapulae laterally and forward.

Sinking the sternum also activates the thymus gland (located behind the upper sternum), an endocrine gland important to the immune system. The process takes place automatically when a person hugs a tree or a big ball. People who are chronic shallow chest breathers with lots of accumulated tension in the chest muscles have very little flexibility in the sternum. When they attempt to sink the chest, the shoulders usually compensate by rising up.

Training in Iron Shirt Chi Kung is a great help in learning to relax the chest and diaphragm. The Packing Breath (taught in Iron Shirt Chi Kung), applied along the different points of the abdomen and up the spine, releases long accumulated tensions and strengthens the muscles, tendons, tissues, and bone marrow.

In addition, the Embracing the Tree position is a perfect blueprint for the Thirteen Movement Tai Chi form. As we shall see in chapter 4, familiarity with Iron Shirt facilitates Tai Chi. That is why, in the Universal Tao, Tai Chi is considered "Iron Shirt in motion."

Rounding the scapulae and sinking the chest are key factors in energy discharge, but they are not the only elements. The position of the feet and knees is what allows the earth energy to begin moving up the legs and into the spine, providing a gentle healing energy to the entire body

ACTIVATE AND ALIGN THE ER CHUI HSIA POINT (T2) AND THE TA CHUI POINT (C7)

The T2 point is located just below the spinous process of the second thoracic vertebra. The seventh cervical vertebrae (C7) is the big spinous process at the base of the neck. The Chinese name for it is *ta chui*, which means "big ver-

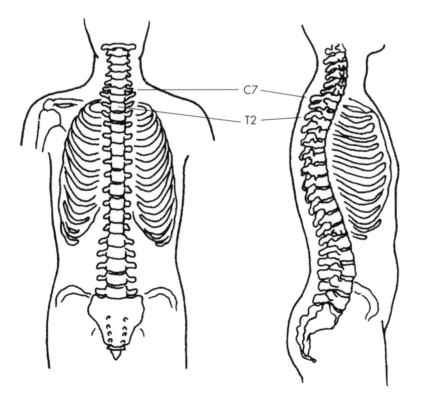

C7

T2

Fig. 3.30 The vertebrae C7 and T2 are the main power points connecting the spine and the arms.

tebrae." In Taoist practice, we regard these bones as the main power points connecting to the arms. All the Yang energy channels of the body meet here. These points are also known as the all-tendon control points. To activate these points, sink the chest, round the scapulae, and gently pull in the chin.

The neck also plays an important role in transferring force from the ground out to the arms. When the neck is not aligned, all the force can jam in the neck and throw off the entire structure.

RELAX THE BODY AND CALM THE MIND

There is an inverse relationship between tension and sensitivity; the more tense a person is, the less sensitive he or she is. When we stay relaxed our senses are more receptive to our opponent. In martial arts it is important to be able to sense where the opponent is weakest and where he or she is strongest. The practitioner can then yield and redirect the brunt of the opponent's force while simultaneously attacking his or her weak and undefended points.

By contrast, when practitioners rely on muscular force their responses are often tense, insensitive, excessive, and inappropriate. They waste their energy confronting the opponent's strength head-on, using force against force, applying maximum effort for minimum results. This is called inefficiency.

The principle of economy in movement arises from a state of internal harmony. A mind that is at peace is not easily swayed or disturbed. This principle also plays a vital role in daily life, whether in business or in combat. When a person overreacts and responds with excessive or unnecessary action, he or she is at a disadvantage.

The basic principle of Tai Chi is to learn how to be relaxed, calm, and mentally clear, whether doing the movements of Tai Chi, doing business, or doing any other activity.

The Tai Chi practitioner is likened to a tiger walking calmly across a meadow but with a perceptible strength. This inner state of calmness and power is enhanced by sitting meditations, such as the Inner Smile and the Microcosmic Orbit, as well the standing meditations of Iron Shirt Chi Kung. Both the sitting and the standing meditations require the physical structure to be aligned so there is no strain. Improper structure can cause tension and make it difficult to relax.

Relaxation is sometimes confused with letting everything go to the point of collapsing the physical and mental structures. This is a wrong perception. Tai Chi is a balance of yin and yang. Therefore the Tai Chi student seeks to release any unnecessary physical and mental tension while at the same time staying mentally alert and physically poised. Relaxing means dropping any physical and mental preoccupation so that the practitioner enters a heightened state of receptivity and openness.

The Tai Chi classics say, "Let go of your own will and follow the will of others." In martial arts, this means that by dropping your preoccupation with your own agenda you become empty, awake, and clear like a mirror, immediately able to perceive when the opponent is about to attack. By staying relaxed and not overreacting, you can respond instantly and appropriately, using the opponent's strength against her or him. Using very little effort, you can join with the chi of your opponent's attack and guide it wherever you want it to go. This is referred to in the Tai Chi classics as "using only four ounces of [your] force to deflect a thousand pounds [of an opponent's force]." This skill can be achieved only by learning to relax, especially in the midst of conflict.

It is best to begin relaxation training in sitting or lying-down meditation. When the body is immobile it is easier to pay attention to dropping physical and mental tensions. Then you can incorporate this relaxation into your Tai Chi; the depth of relaxation experienced in meditation is carried over into a wide range of motions.

Any bodily movement involves muscular contractions and releases. It is impossible to move your physical structure without tensing and contracting whole series of muscles and tendons. The challenge in Tai Chi is to execute all the movements without tensing or tightening to the point of interfering with the energy flow, and in learning to release once the movement ceases so as to feel the newly gained chi. This is called Wu Wei, effortlessness, using minimum effort to achieve maximum results. The Taoist classics are full of references to Wu Wei, yet nowhere is it better demonstrated than in the gentle, flowing movements of Tai Chi.

In another part of the Tai Chi classics it is stated, "Use mind, not force." When the Yi, the mind-eye-heart, guides the chi, the blood and body structure are moved without overly depending on the muscles. The energetic expense is minimal, and internally one feels more at ease.

CLEARLY DISTINGUISH YIN AND YANG

Just as in the universe, where all manifestation is an interplay of yin and yang, all the movements of Tai Chi are a constant interplay of yin and yang. Without yin and yang, active and passive, there is no movement. Tai Chi practice re-creates this process of cosmic expression through the sequence of movements.

Fig. 3.31 The Tai Chi symbol: yin and yang   **Fig. 3.32** Yin and yang movement

The primordial state of Wu Chi is expressed in the first posture of standing still, totally centered and balanced—unmanifested. The moment the legs are separated and we begin to move, the process of yin and yang becomes active. In Tai Chi, yin and yang are understood primarily in terms of substantial (yang) and insubstantial (yin). This is what creates the flow of the energy.

Substantial (yang) is a relative term in Tai Chi. It refers to the most active element of the movement. In terms of the legs, it can mean that all or most of the weight is on one foot. In terms of the arms, it can mean that one arm is in front and is discharging energy through a punch or push. *Insubstantial* (yin) refers to the other arm or leg, which is playing the supportive and stabilizing role at the moment.

In terms of advancing and sinking back, an advance is yang and sinking back is yin. In terms of the breath, inhaling is yin and exhaling is yang. Raising the arms is yang; lowering them is yin. The weight is constantly shifting from one leg to the other. At the same time, one hand and arm are dominant while the other hand and arm play a supportive role. Just as with the legs, the active arm is constantly changing.

The awareness of substantial and insubstantial has a very practical purpose beyond martial arts applications. Once the body learns to move by constantly flowing from empty to full, from full to empty, it becomes apparent that these

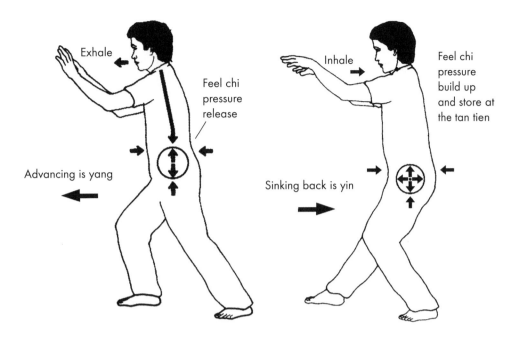

Fig. 3.33 Exhale and push forward: yang   **Fig. 3.34** Inhale and sink back: yin

same principles can be applied to social endeavors, personal relationships, careers, and politics. The practitioner discovers how to work effectively with yin and yang, discerning when to yield and when to advance in daily life.

COORDINATE INNER AND OUTER, MIND AND BODY

Another rule of energy circulation is that the life force follows the intention of the mind-eye-heart. The Tai Chi classics say, "The mind intention leads and the chi follows; the chi leads and the body follows." Thus, if the intention of the mind is to move the right arm down, the life force will aid in that movement of the arm.

The Tai Chi Classics also say, "Use mind intention, not muscular force." By using the mind-eye-heart to move the chi, we move with a minimum of effort. In Tai Chi we learn to move using just the right amount of energy needed to accomplish the purpose: neither too much nor too little, neither too early nor too late.

One of the basic principles of Tai Chi is to move in coordinated continuous sequences, with all parts of the body connected and working together harmoniously. This continuous flow manifests through the physical structure as gracefulness and through the mental structure as emotional balance and

Fig. 3.35 Moving the structure as a unit

steadiness of character; this is what we call integrity. That the word *integrity* is rarely used nowadays reflects the imbalance of our mental and emotional structures, our lack of integration.

Attaining an integrated structure is a repair process that takes place at several levels. The most basic level is the energy flow in the body. When the life force is unable to circulate unimpeded, automatically some areas of the body will be affected with too much energy or too little. This is reflected in our thinking, our emotions, and the way we move.

We discussed previously how emotional and mental states manifest in the physical structure. Negative emotional energy inhibits movement. Over time, emotions begin to be held in the muscles, organs, and tissues, creating tightness and restricted movement. The Microcosmic Orbit meditation opens these energy blockages by restoring energy flow.

Without mental balance and emotional stability, the Tai Chi practitioner often struggles in vain trying to move in one piece. Without the help of meditation, it might take many years of Tai Chi practice to attain the state of mental and emotional balance that results in physical integrity. The emotions of joy, anger, fear, sadness, worry, love, respect, and so on are the most powerful forms of energy ordinarily experienced. Fully expressing the emotions is one characteristic of a dynamic and integrated personality.

A person should not be at the mercy of the emotions, however. The

Fusion of the Five Elements meditation is one of the most powerful methods for regulating the emotions and recycling any excess emotional energy back into balanced life force energy. The Taoist experiences emotions fully and then allows them to flow on once the situation that provoked them is finished. Regular practice of the Fusion Meditation gradually creates a state of emotional balance and integrity that manifests as solidity of character and inner strength.

Through the practice of Tai Chi, this emotional state is expressed as integrated movements animated from within. Each movement becomes the manifestation of the mind, body, and spirit moving as one.

Learning to move the structure in one piece has many subtle levels of refinement. Ordinarily we move using a combination of muscles, tendons, and bones but with little conscious emphasis on using our chi. In Tai Chi the situation is totally reversed. As practitioners become more and more acquainted with the life force through sitting, standing, and moving meditation, they are able to sense very clearly the energy moving within the limbs and trunk. One of the rules of energy circulation is that the more relaxed a person is, the more easily the energy is able to circulate. For the Tai Chi practitioner, the first challenge is to relax as much as possible in each move and to feel inner calm and strength so that the energy can circulate as fast as possible. The next level of subtlety is allowing the movements to flow from the life force rather than from the mechanical contraction of muscles, bones, and tendons.

The life force circulates through the body along the meridians. Thus, the prerequisite for moving animated by life force is to open the channels. Once again, a background in meditation provides a solid foundation for entering this subtle stage of Tai Chi. One of the results of allowing the life force to empower the movements is that the chi can flow like a river. This enables the practitioner to move smoothly and continuously, without sudden shifts in tempo.

Warm-Up Exercises and Preparation

Whether you are a Tai Chi student or an expert, practice is essential. A practice session can be fruitless, however, if the body is not properly prepared to handle the energy it is about to absorb. This is the main reason for the additional Tai Chi training exercises elucidated in this chapter. To warm up for Tai Chi means to activate the chi and blood flow and invigorate their circulation throughout the body. Warm-up exercises are particularly important for areas of the body that are rarely stretched, such as the spine and the sacrum. Even a person who does muscular and aerobic workouts is still not properly prepared for the conduction of large amounts of energy. Without an adequate warm-up before exercise, the muscles may also be stiff, tight, and lacking in sufficient blood supply to meet the sudden demands placed on them by strenuous activity. This is one of the major causes of athletic injury.

Following is a series of special exercises that enhance the body's receptivity and the mind's acuity to the practice of Tai Chi. The Universal Tao warm-up exercises are gentle yet effective. They are easy to learn, and you will discover that they are also easy to perform.

Listen to the messages from your body as you do the various exercises. Pain is the body's warning signal that you may be overdoing it. The goal is not to go to extremes in stretching or to develop major muscles; instead, the aim is to loosen the joints and relax the muscles so the chi and blood can flow without obstruction. Don't force yourself to your limits; less is better, especially at the beginning. If you feel any joint pain or discomfort doing any of the exercises, back off until it feels comfortable. If you still feel strain or pain, discontinue the exercise altogether.

Be especially respectful of any injuries, chronic problems, or physical limitations you may have. When you are kind and gentle to your body, it starts to trust you and begins to relax by itself. You will find yourself starting to loosen up on a deeper level without having to force the issue. In this way you will develop naturally, gradually, and safely.

In Tai Chi you learn to reorganize the way in which you move. In particular, you discover how to coordinate all of your movements from your center and how to use the power of the waist and the lower tan tien to move in a strong, stable, integrated way. You will see that many of the warm-up movements focus on training the waist for this reason.

Fig. 4.1 Waist Loosening

Waist Loosening

1. Stand with the feet parallel, slightly wider than shoulder-width apart. Allow the arms to dangle loosely at your sides.
2. Begin to turn the hips from side to side. Let the arms swing naturally and easily with the momentum of the hips turning. Explore your natural and comfortable range of hip motion. Don't go to extremes; just stay within your free and easy comfort zone.
3. After turning just the hips ten or twelve times, allow the lumbar vertebrae to relax and loosen and gently twist with the hips. You should still begin the movement from the hips, but now allow the lumbar vertebrae to respond as well.
4. Next allow the middle spine, upper back, and neck to twist gently with the movement.
5. Keep the shoulders loose and let the arms swing with the movement. Don't use effort to move the arms; let them be totally limp and just let the

body swing them. At the same time, be aware of the gentle twisting of the knee and ankle joints as you twist the whole body. Do this at least thirty-six times to each side.

🌀 Opening the Door of Life

1. Begin in the same stance as for Waist Loosening. This time twist to the left, again initiating the movement from the hips. Let the right arm swing across the front of the torso, raising it up to head height with the palm facing away from you. At the same time, let the left arm swing around to the back and place the back of the left hand over the Door of Life, the area on the spine opposite the navel.

2. When you reach your full extension, relax, and then extend again by loosening the lower back. Feel the gentle stretch and increased extension coming all the way from the Door of Life, not from the shoulders. Relax and extend in this way three times.

3. Twist to the right and repeat the steps as above on the right side. Repeat for a total of nine times on each side.

Fig. 4.2 Opening the Door of Life

🌀 Windmill Exercise: Opening the Spinal Joints

Practice each phase of this exercise slowly and mindfully.

Outer Front Extension

1. Begin in the same stance as for Waist Loosening. Bring the hands to the midline of the body and hook the thumbs together.

Fig. 4.3 Windmill Exercise opening position

2. Keeping the hands close to the torso, inhale and raise the arms until they are extended straight up over the head, the fingers pointing up. Gently stretch upward in this position, extending the spine slightly backward. You can even say "Ah-h-h-h-h," as you would when you stretch first thing in the morning.

3. Begin to exhale slowly and bend forward, reaching as far out in front as you can, keeping the head between the arms. Try to feel the joints of the spine releasing one by one in a wavelike motion. Bend first from the lumbar vertebrae, then from the thoracic vertebrae, and finally from the cervical vertebrae. At this point your spine is released all the way toward the floor.

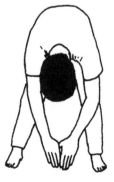

Fig. 4.4 Outer Front Extension movements down

Fig. 4.5 Outer Front Extension movements up

4. Slowly straighten back up, again feeling each joint of the spine, from the sacrum and lumbar area through the thorax and the neck and base of the skull. Keep the arms hanging heavily and let the head be the last part of the body to come to vertical. Now you are back in the stretching position.
5. Repeat this movement three to five times. Finish with the arms overhead, as at the end of step 2.

Inner Front Extension

1. Now do the same movements in reverse. Point the fingertips down toward the floor and slowly lower the arms, keeping the hands close to the torso. When the arms are completely lowered, begin to bend forward; release the head, the cervical vertebrae, the thoracic vertebrae, and the lumbar vertebrae until you are bent all the way forward, as at the end of step 3 of the Outer Front Extension. Feel each joint opening.

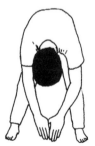

Fig. 4.6 Inner Front Extension movements down

Fig. 4.7 Inner Front Extension movements up

2. Keeping the head between the arms, begin to straighten up. Feel each joint of the spine, from the sacrum and lumbar area through the thorax and the neck and base of the skull. This time let the arms extend out in front as you slowly stand erect. When you come to vertical, the arms will be straight against the head.

3. Gently stretch upward in this position, extending the spine slightly back. Say "Ah-h-h-h-h," as you would when you stretch first thing in the morning.

4. Repeat three to five times.

Left Sidebending

1. Begin standing erect, feet shoulder-width apart. With your head between your arms in the overhead position, lean to the left. You should feel a gentle stretch on the left side of the waist.

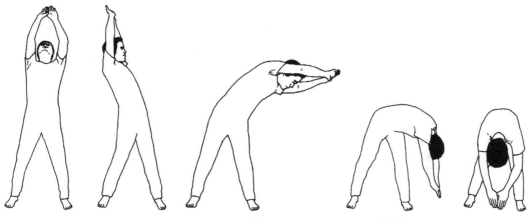

Fig. 4.8 Sidebending movements to the left

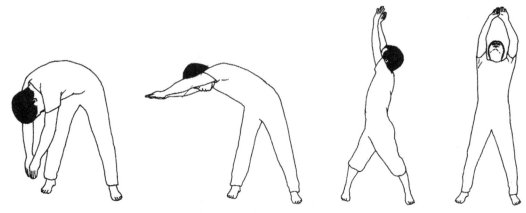

Fig. 4.9 Sidebending movements to the right

2. Continue stretching to the side until you've reached your limit, then gently rotate toward center as you stretch all the way down to the floor.
3. From center, circle back up on the right side until you are again standing straight with the arms overhead.
4. Repeat three to five times, bending left to center and returning on the right.

Right Sidebending and Conclusion

1. Repeat the same movements as in the Left Sidebending, but this time begin bending to the right side and return on the left side.
2. Repeat three to five times.
3. To finish, unhook the thumbs and let the arms slowly float back down to the sides.

Fig. 4.10 Completion

⟳ Tendon-Twisting Exercises

In these exercises the tendons of the wrists, elbows, and shoulders are stretched and twisted to enhance both flexibility and power. The movements should feel as though you are turning a screw into a wall.

Fig. 4.11 Small Tendon Twist

Fig. 4.12 Small Tendon Twist in reverse

Small Tendon Twist

1. Begin standing erect, feet shoulder-width apart. Reach forward with both arms, palms up. Using a circular screwing motion, twist both thumbs so they face downward. Then reverse directions and circle the hands forward, returning to the starting position. While doing this, the wrists and elbows should be fully torqued to the point where, if you listen carefully, you can actually hear the stretching of the tendons that are being affected. The shoulders should be relaxed and rounded.

2. Repeat three to nine times.

3. Now repeat this movement with both arms above the head, with arms at the sides, and with both arms in front of the body but down at the groin.

4. Repeat three to nine times in each position.

5. Now repeat in all positions, but reverse the direction of the tendon twist.

Large Tendon Twist

1. This exercise comprises the same movements as Small Tendon Twist but it is performed in large circles. This movement should be practiced only in the front of the body.

2. Do three to nine rounds of Large Tendon Twist.

3. Repeat the movements, reversing the direction of the tendon twist and joint opening. Practice three to nine rounds in this direction.

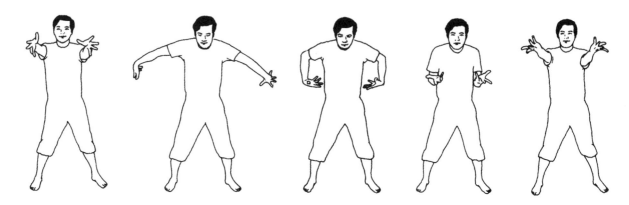

Fig. 4.13 Large Tendon Twist

🌀 Head Rotations and Neck-Joint Opening

1. Stand erect, your hands on your hips. Let the head relax forward. Feel the weight of the head providing a gentle stretch to the back of the neck. Allow the weight of the head to provide all the loosening and stretching force; it helps you relax and release and avoids the risk of injury from overstraining.

2. Gently roll the head to the right and feel the stretch on the left side of the neck.

3. Feeling the weight of the head, gently roll the head to the back. Feel the stretch on the front of the neck.

4. Gently roll the head to the left, feeling the stretch on the right side of the neck.

Fig. 4.14 Head Rotations

5. Repeat steps 1 through 4 two more times, and then repeat the sequence three times in the opposite direction.

Shoulder Rotations and Joint Opening

This exercise increases your scapular power. Many people, especially those with a strong back, develop knots of tension in the shoulders. In this exercise the scapulae are loosened and rounded to develop the kind of scapular power used by tigers and other big cats.

1. Begin by standing with the feet parallel and slightly wider than shoulder-width apart. Relax the entire body, paying special attention to relaxing the shoulders, scapulae, and back. Keep the palms loosely on the front of the thighs throughout this exercise.
2. Lift the shoulders straight up.
3. Extend the shoulders forward.
4. Lower the shoulders downward.
5. Draw the shoulders back.

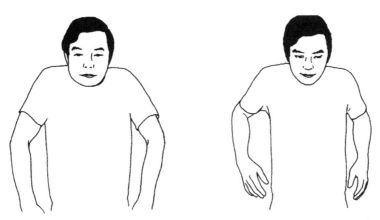

Fig. 4.15 Shoulder Rotations

6. Repeat steps 2 through 5 eight more times.

7. Now reverse direction: raise the shoulders, draw them back, lower them, and bring them forward.

8. Repeat nine times.

Hip Rotations

1. Stand with the feet parallel and slightly wider than shoulder-width apart. Place the hands on the waist. As you perform Hip Rotations, keep the head positioned over the feet—don't jut the jaw and head forward or let the head fall behind the centerline of the body. Move slowly and easily, breathing deeply and continuously.

2. Bring the hips forward.

3. Move the hips in a big circle toward the right.

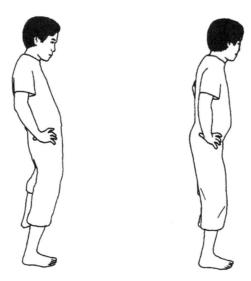

Fig. 4.16 Hip Rotations

4. Now move the hips in a circle toward the back.

5. Circle the hips toward the left.

6. Repeat steps 2 through 5 eight more times.

7. Reverse direction and repeat steps 2 through 5 nine times.

Knee Rotations

1. Stand erect with the feet together. Bend the knees and place the palms lightly on the kneecaps.

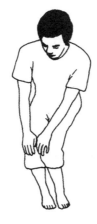

Fig. 4.17 Knee Rotations

2. Slowly and gently rotate the knees to the left.
3. Rotate the knees to the back. The muscles behind the knees will lengthen.
4. Rotate the knees to the right.
5. Repeat steps 2 through 4 eight more times.
6. Now reverse direction and repeat nine times.

Ankle/Knee/Hip Rotations and Joint Opening

Keeping the joints open is an important part of allowing the energy to be properly stored and available to flow into the bones. This exercise helps open the joints and flex the tendons so you do not overstress them during Tai Chi practice.

1. Stand erect with your hands on your hips, feet together. Raise the right leg and begin to rotate the right ankle clockwise nine to thirty-six times.
2. Now rotate the ankle counterclockwise the same number of times.
3. Keeping the leg raised, rotate the foreleg from the knee in a clockwise circular motion nine to thirty-six times.
4. Now rotate the foreleg the same number of times counterclockwise.
5. Finally, rotate the entire leg from the hip joint in a clockwise circular motion nine to thirty-six times.
6. Rotate the leg the same number of times counterclockwise.
7. Repeat the sequence with the left leg raised.

Fig. 4.18 Ankle Rotations

🌀 Tan Tien Hitting

Since the lower tan tien is the major storage center for the chi of the body, this area should be activated prior to Tai Chi practice.

1. Stand with the feet parallel and slightly wider than shoulder-width apart. Totally relax the arms and gracefully swing them in free fall from left to right. As you swing to the left, the right hand comes in front of the body, with the palm hitting the navel area at the exact same time that the back of the left hand hits the Door of Life, opposite the navel.
2. As you swing to the right the left hand comes in front of the body, with the palm hitting the navel area at the exact same time as the back of the right hand hits the Door of Life.
3. Repeat thirty-six times to each side.

Fig. 4.19 Tan Tien Hitting

Bouncing and Shaking the Joints

Bouncing the body can likened to a ride on the subway. For those of you who commute this way, this exercise can be practiced to and from work as well.

1. Stand with the feet parallel and slightly wider than shoulder-width apart. Relax the body and concentrate on opening the joints.
2. Now bounce without any tension. Let the vibration in the heels work its way up through the entire skeletal system, from legs to spine to neck to skull. Shoulders and arms vibrate as the arms hang loosely out to the side or down by the sides of the body. To enhance the vibration you can hum a vowel, which will make the voice tremble as well.
3. Rest and feel chi entering the joints.

Fig. 4.20 Bouncing

Energy-Connection Exercises

To the average person who is not familiar with Tai Chi, when we say that we are going to practice gathering, directing, and storing energy, the first question that may be asked is, "What energy?" Here is a series of exercises that not only prepare the body for connecting with that energy, but also enhance the mind/eye/heart connection.

Washing the Body with Heavenly and Earth Energy

1. Stand in the Embracing the Tree position: The feet are shoulder-and-a-half-width apart, the nine points of the feet pressing firmly against the

ground. The knees are bent and torqued slightly outward with a corresponding torque in the ankles and hips. This acts to screw the body into the ground and to initiate the earth connection. Straighten the spine by slightly tucking the sacrum (this increases the connection to the earth) and by tucking in the chin to connect with the heavenly energy. Round the scapulae, sink the chest, and hold the head erect. Position the arms as if they were encircling a tree, keeping the elbows sunk.

2. Reach down and forward, keeping the palms cupped, and slowly scoop the earth energy up through your body. Use your imagination at first, until you become sensitized to the feeling of the rising earth energy. Since you are washing your body with this energy, simultaneously feel a cool, blue waterlike healing sensation rising through the body at the level of the hands as you raise them up, lifting them until they are fully extended above the head.

Fig. 4.21 Washing the Body

3. Turn the palms up and connect with the heavenly energy.
4. Slowly arc the arms downward to the sides, palms out. Feel heavenly energy descend through the body at the level of the hands. The heavenly energy may feel like a hot, white, firelike, expansive sensation that washes down through the body until it reaches the ground, at which point the hands will be reaching toward the ground.
5. Repeat this exercise nine to thirty-six times, until you feel fully suffused with both earth energy and heavenly energy.

Fig. 4.22 Gathering the heavenly forces

Cosmic Energy Mid-Eyebrow Connection

This exercise should be performed only at night, or at sunrise or sunset, when the light of the sun is softer and will not damage your eyes. Close and rest your eyes if ever the light from the sun or the moon feels too intense.

1. Begin in the Embracing the Tree position as described in step 1 of Washing the Body on page 71, but this time face the sun or the moon.

2. Bring up the arms to just above the level of the mid-eyebrow and make a triangle between the index fingers and thumbs of both hands, with either the sun or the moon centered within the triangle.

3. Hold this position and draw in the sun (yang) or moon (yin) energy through the mid-eyebrow.

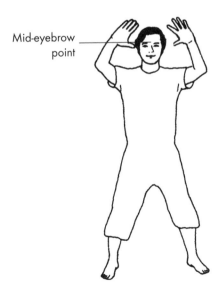

Mid-eyebrow
point

Fig. 4.23 Opening the mid-eyebrow

4. Gather some saliva in your mouth and let the energy of the sun or the moon that you've drawn in mix with the saliva to collect a ball of chi energy in the mouth. This will increase saliva production and more will gather in the mouth.

5. Slightly extend the neck. Swallow the saliva with a strong gulp and mentally direct it to the navel. Feel the navel warm with the arrival of this new energy.

6. Do these steps from nine to thirty-six times.

7. Close the exercise by slowly lowering the arms to the navel, placing the left hand over the right, and collecting energy by spiraling at the navel.

Navel/Palm Connection

1. Stand tall with the feet slightly wider than shoulder-width apart. Position both palms approximately two inches out from the navel, palms facing inward.

2. Slowly inhale, allowing the abdomen to expand completely. As this is happening, lilghtly tug a "string" of energy away from the navel, using the centers of the palms.

3. Now slowly exhale and feed the energy string back in to the navel.

4. Do this sequence nine times, and then collect energy at the navel.

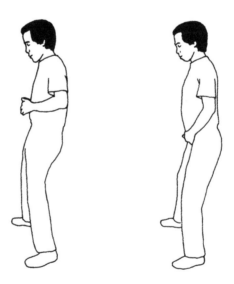

Fig. 4.24 Opening the navel

Sink Back and Push Tree

1. Find a tree that beckons you with its positive energy. Selecting the proper tree is vital, since there are trees with negative energy.
2. Facing the tree with the right leg forward, sink into the Tài Chi Sink Back position. The fingers face the tree.
3. As you proceed forward into the push, feel a connection as the energy from the fingertips shoots out and connects with the positive energy of the tree. Project out from your body any sick or negative emotions. Let those energies be taken in by the tree, to be healed and recycled through the earth.
4. Sink back and draw in the newly processed positive energy.
5. Do this yin and yang action nine, eighteen, or thirty-six times. This exercise is particularly effective for energy sensitization.

Fig. 4.25 Tree connection

⟳ Structure Exercises

The following exercises build structural power and strength. Once the energy can flow, it is important that your body structure is properly aligned to feed that energy into the various conduits and sites where the body needs healing and strengthening. These exercises emphasize opening and developing the structure in specific areas so that the energy is able to flow properly.

Single-Leg Stance with Raised Arm

The connection between heaven and earth through the human body is one of the main concepts in Tài Chi practice. But this force can only flow with strength if the channels are properly opened. To ensure that one side of the

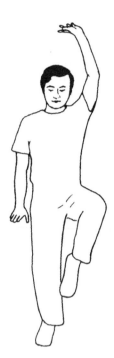

Fig. 4.26 Leg and arm raising

body is not more open than the other, and to achieve a balance between the left (yin) side and the right (yang) side, this exercise allows the heavenly force to flow in to the hand on one side of the body and then out to the earth on the other side. This creates balance and opens the channel by temporarily removing weight from the opposite leg and arm, so that you double the force on one side that is ordinarily divided between the limbs.

1. Begin by standing on the right leg with the left leg bent and raised, to prevent any flow through it. Raise the left arm, palm up, and leave the right arm relaxed at the side.

2. Draw the heavenly force in to the palm of your left hand. Feel the energy flow through the arm and across the torso and then out the right leg into the earth. This posture will test and improve your balance. Maintain this position for as long as possible, building up to three minutes.

3. Now switch and repeat the exercise on the opposite side. Try to do both sides of the body for an equal length of time so as to properly balance their flow.

Dog Holding Leg: Opening the Spinal Joints

Not all the Iron Shirt exercises are taught in detail in this book; however, for readers who know how to do the Turtle, this is an exercise that can apply to Tai Chi.

1. From the Turtle position, wrap the right arm around the right leg. Pass the left arm between the legs and clasp the right forearm.
2. Slowly pulling upward, arch the back and feel the current flowing from the spine through the legs and into the earth.
3. Repeat on the opposite side.
4. Finally, bending the knees a bit more, wrap both arms around both legs and clasp the right arm at the forearm with the left hand. Again, pulling up as if lifting yourself, arch the back to create a strong energy flow throughout the skeletal system.

Fig. 4.27 Dog Holding Leg posture

Opening the Groin (Kua)

Opening the kua makes for strong engagement of the psoas muscles (see page 46). As you do this exercise, pay close attention to deeply relaxing and lengthening the psoas muscles.

1. Stand with your feet parallel and shoulder-width apart. Place a hand on your inguinal crease, the crease at your groin.
2. Arch your back slightly, tilting your sacrum back. Then slightly tuck your sacrum forward and sink your pelvis, as if you were going to sit down in a chair without bending your knees. You will feel the inguinal crease deepen. Focus on feeling the movement of the ball-and-socket joints of the hips and femurs. The joints will feel as if they are inflating inside as they fill with chi.
3. Begin to transfer the energetic force to the heels. As you feel the energy travel downward, open and spiral the knee joints outward. You will feel that same sensation of the joints opening and inflating as they fill with chi.

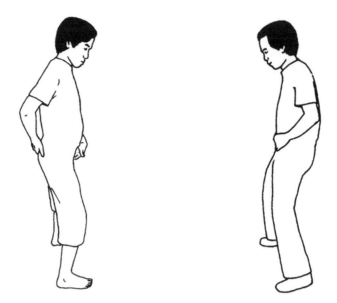

Fig. 4.28 Moving the sacrum

4. Transfer the force to the heels and feel them open and fill with chi.

5. Now feel the force gently rebound from the earth up through the heels to the sacrum. Feel the area between the sacrum and lumbar spine expand and fill with chi. Feel the force transfer up the spine to the Door of Life as the chi enters the spine, and feel the entire spine lengthening and straightening.

 Power Exercises

The previous set of exercises distinguishes Tai Chi from most other forms of exercise in that the emphasis is placed on feeling energy and opening the channels for the chi to move. In the next series of exercises, power is recognized not as muscular but instead as a result of using the structure of the body in conjunction with the energy to produce great force.

Stork Exercise

1. Begin by standing on your right leg, your left leg bent and raised like a stork. Your arms are long, palms facing down.

2. With arms fully extended, sink in the groin/kua, then slowly bend your right leg, lowering your body down to the point where your palms rest on the floor. It is likely that you won't be able to make it all the way to the floor at first; just bend as low as possible. Your upper body must remain

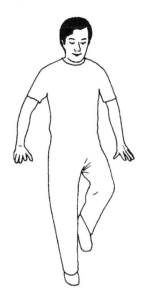

Fig. 4.29 Stork Exercise

erect with your muscles relaxed. Sink first in the groin/kua area before bending your knees.

3. Raise your body back up by using the force of your right leg to lengthen and straighten itself.

4. Do this exercise nine or eighteen times.

5. Then repeat the sequence on the left leg, with the right leg raised.

Medicine Ball Practice

There are a few older Tai Chi practices that, in addition to the body, use props. One of these props is called a medicine ball; it is a heavy ball used to provide extra resistance in the practice of the tan tien motion. Practice with the medicine ball involves lying down and placing the ball on the abdomen, then breathing with the intention of moving the ball up and down. This helps to develop strength in the lower body.

Heavy Stick Exercise

Another of the older practices with props is the Heavy Stick Exercise. By practicing the Tai Chi motion with a heavy wooden or iron pole over the shoulders, you increase strength in the legs and waist.

Warm-Up Exercises and Preparation

79

Fig. 4.30 Heavy Stick Exercise

Groin Weight Lifting

Finally, an important aspect of both the higher-level meditations and the Tai Chi form is the Groin Weight Lifting exercises. While the details of this exercise are fully described in my *Bone Marrow Nei Kung* book, **[ed]** it is worth mentioning here. The power of the groin and the relationship of the groin with the internal organs are greatly strengthened through the use of this technique. Additionally, the practice helps you better connect with the planets in the Tai Chi Healing Form described in chapter 12.

Sole and Heel Press

1. Position yourself in the Tai Chi front stance with the back (left) foot turned out at a 45-degree angle and the front (right) leg bent.
2. Bend your left knee, shift your weight back, and practice pressing from the sole to the heel of the back foot to send the body and earth energy bouncing forward. It is important that, while you feel the spring of the energy like a horse leaping, you still perform this pressing movement slowly to let the power manifest when the weight of the body shifts from the back leg to the front leg.
3. Press from sole to heel from eighteen to thirty-six times to gain a powerful forward motion.
4. Repeat on the opposite side.

5. Next, starting from the forward position, use the ball of the front foot to press down in order to move the body in a controlled backward motion into the sink position. Again, the energy of the foot and sole initiates the motion; the rest of the motion is controlled by the slow transfer of weight from the front to the back leg.

6. Do this motion eighteen or thirty-six times. Then repeat on the opposite side.

7. Finally, combine the forward and backward motions in one powerful movement. Practice on both the left and right side for eighteen or thirty-six times each side.

Low Stance Tai Chi Practice

Once you have mastered the power exercises described here, it is important to optimize this power in your Tai Chi practice. This is done by performing the Tai Chi Chi Kung form in a low stance. Through bending the knees and widening the stance, the low practice of Tai Chi can enhance the ability to use the form in martial applications and self-defense. The increased force on the tendons of the ankles and knees further enhances your power.

Be sure to keep your body upright in your lower-stance practice, and take care that your front knee does not extend beyond your toes in the forward stance.

Fig. 4.32 Low Stance Tai Chi Practice

ENERGETIC PREPARATIONS FOR TAI CHI CHI KUNG

To master Tai Chi Chi Kung you must also master the fundamental Taoist energy practices. These practices include the Inner Smile, the Microcosmic Orbit Meditation, Iron Shirt Chi Kung, and the Six Healing Sounds.

Appendix 1 of this book presents a simplified version of these practices. For in-depth guidance, readers should receive personal instruction from a certified Universal Tao Instructor. In addition, readers may refer to our books, videotapes, and audiocassettes for further information.

Although it may seem at first as if there are so many practices that there could never be enough hours in the day to do them all, once you gain skill in each practice you will find that you can perform them quickly and still get excellent results. You can then incorporate them all into your daily round of Tai Chi practice.

It is not always necessary to practice all the preparatory energetic exercises before performing each round of Tai Chi Chi Kung. You can distribute your practice throughout the day. There is no question, however, that if you precede your Tai Chi practice with a round of the Inner Smile, the Microcosmic Orbit, and Embracing the Tree, your Tai Chi will reach a more profound level.

Some people prefer to do their seated Inner Smile and Microcosmic Orbit meditation after practicing Tai Chi Chi Kung. They find that the warm-up movements, standing meditation, and Tai Chi make their bodies more open and supple, and it then becomes easier for them to relax and go deeper into their meditation. The way of the Tao is to find your own rhythm and determine what works best for you.

Having learned the warm-up and preparatory foundation practices, you are now ready to proceed to the Tai Chi Chi Kung form itself.

Tai Chi Chi Kung Thirteen Movement Form

The thirteen postures of Tai Chi are movements identified by original Tai Chi practitioners. They include yin and yang defense moves and yang attacking motions as well as centering or finding equilibrium. The name Thirteen Movement Form comes to us through history and is not to be taken literally in trying to find a one-to-one correspondence with the form taught here.

Beginners and older people generally practice the Tai Chi Chi Kung Thirteen Movement form with a higher stance. As the student progresses, he or she can practice with a middle-structure stance, one that is closer to the ground, to increase strength. For martial purposes the practitioner generally uses an extremely low stance.

INTRODUCTORY MOVEMENTS

The first movement of the Tai Chi form is internal, not external. Outwardly, you are standing still, facing north. This position is related to Wu Chi, the primordial unmanifested state.

🌀 Wu Chi Stance

1. The feet are close together but not touching at the ankles. The nine points of the feet make contact with the ground. This is the root, the connecting point with earth energy. The knees are extended but not locked. The back

is straight and relaxed. No pressure, tension, or pain should be felt in the lumbar area.

2. The shoulders are relaxed, with the head pulled upward at the crown. This is the heavenly pull that draws the earth energy up through the feet. Feel the heavenly pull, as if a chi ball above your head is pulling you up. The pull also stretches the spine, allowing the energy to circulate more freely. At the same time feel the chi enter the coccyx and straighten the spine.

3. The eyes are open without strain. The focus is directly ahead, to the horizon. The chin is pulled back slightly. This subtle movement backward opens the base of the skull area so the energy can circulate freely up to the crown and down the front.

4. The tongue tip is touching the palate lightly at a point that helps induce salivation. The jaw is relaxed with the teeth lightly touching. Clenching the jaw brings tension to the sides of the head and the throat, which you don't want to feel. The throat is relaxed. Swallowing a little saliva and exhaling gently relaxes the muscles of the neck.

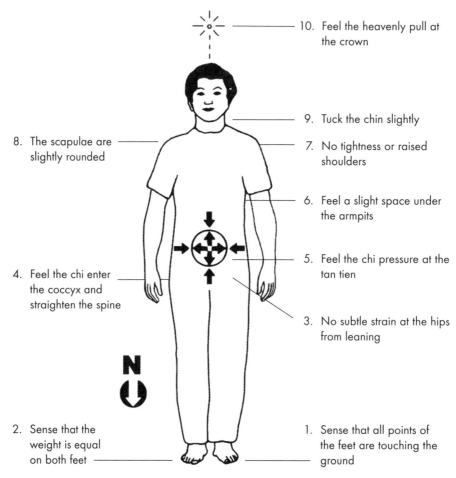

10. Feel the heavenly pull at the crown

9. Tuck the chin slightly

8. The scapulae are slightly rounded

7. No tightness or raised shoulders

6. Feel a slight space under the armpits

5. Feel the chi pressure at the tan tien

4. Feel the chi enter the coccyx and straighten the spine

3. No subtle strain at the hips from leaning

2. Sense that the weight is equal on both feet

1. Sense that all points of the feet are touching the ground

Fig. 5.1 Wu Chi stance

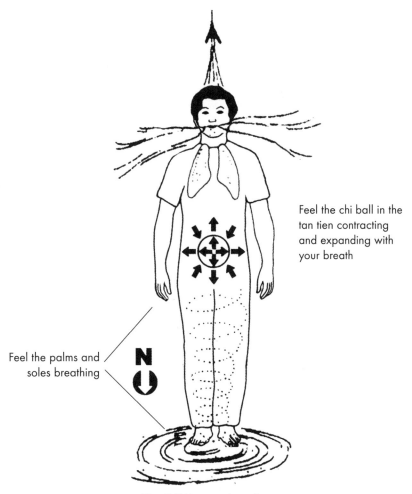

Feel the chi ball in the tan tien contracting and expanding with your breath

Feel the palms and soles breathing

N

Fig. 5.2 Tan tien breathing

5. The chest is relaxed and slightly hollowed. This hollowing is produced by a subtle rounding of the scapulae. If the chest is tight, you can relax it by inhaling gently without making noise and then exhaling just as quietly through parted lips.

6. The breath is even and deep, expanding the abdomen. The attention is at the navel, or at the lower tan tien, the point deep to the navel and close to the kidneys. The breath penetrates to this tan tien, creating the sensation of a growing energy ball.

7. The arms are relaxed with a hollow in the armpits, as if holding a Ping-Pong ball there. The arms are not touching the body. The palms of both hands are relaxed and the fingers are loose yet straight. The index fingers are very slightly raised; feel energy sparkling at the tips of the fingers.

8. Once you are organized and internally present in this movement, smile down to the thymus gland, behind the upper sternum. Allow the smile to

Tai Chi Chi Kung Thirteen Movement Form

spread to the heart and all other organs. Smile down to the navel. Listen to the heartbeat. Follow the pulse from the heart out through the chest, shoulders, upper arms, elbows, forearms, wrists, hands, and fingers. Feel the pulse in the index and pinkie fingers.

9. Become aware of the earth energy at your feet, the heavenly pull at the crown, and the cosmic energy in the front of your body. Inhale gently without making noise and draw the cosmic energy in to the mid-eyebrow. Let the cosmic energy penetrate deeply to the lungs, spread to all the organs, and fill the soles of the feet.

10. When the inhalation is completed, retain the breath for a moment, without straining, and then begin to exhale gently without making noise. If a piece of paper were placed in front of the nostrils, it would not move with the air being exhaled.

Opening Tai Chi

Preparation: Step Out

1. With the exhalation begin to sink down, shifting the weight onto the right leg. The sinking should originate from the hips and sacrum, so that you are sinking and folding at the groin (the kua) without much of a bend in the knees and can feel the weight transfer down the back of the knees to the heels. Sinking by simply bending the knees puts too much stress on them, resulting in swelling and injury.

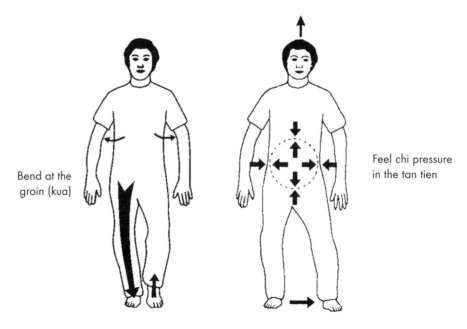

Bend at the groin (kua)

Feel chi pressure in the tan tien

Fig. 5.3 Preparation, part 1   **Fig. 5.4** Preparation, part 2

The arms come out slightly from the sides by sinking the chest and rounding the scapulae a bit. Rotate the hands so that the palms face back. The energy flows through the arms down to the palms and fingertips. As the chest sinks the sternum moves inward, massaging the thymus gland.

The crown remains aligned with the heavenly force, so there is no leaning to compensate for sinking down on the right leg.

Once all the weight is on the right leg, inhale as you lift the left heel, keeping the big toe touching the ground.

2. Separate the legs by brushing the ground lightly toward the left with the big toe, as if tracing a line (fig. 5.4). The separation between the two feet is roughly the width of the shoulders. This is the base. When the space between the two feet is less than shoulder width, the base is narrower than the top, resulting in a top-heavy structure. In this style of Tai Chi the base is not wider than the shoulders' width.

Exhale as you place the left foot firmly on the ground, all nine points touching the ground, and shift the weight so that it is equally on both feet. The knees remain slightly bent but not extending over the edge of the toes.

The pelvic area is open. Feel the energy ball in the navel area. The spine feels stretched by the heavenly pull upward; the sacrum feels as though it's being pulled downward by the earth force.

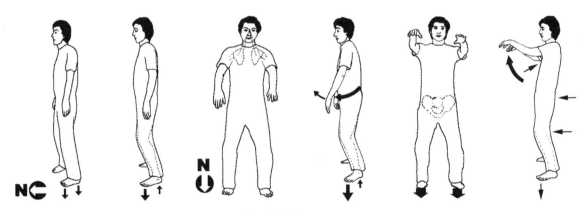

Fig. 5.5 Raise arms

Raise the Arms

1. First rock slightly forward. This movement is almost imperceptible—the nine points of the feet remain glued to the ground. Now rock back and sink the coccyx until you feel the feet connect even more firmly to the earth.

2. Allow the momentum of the earth force rising up to the scapulae to begin raising the arms. Begin your inhalation as you start to raise the arms. As

you raise the arms, make sure they remain bent at the elbows. The palms of the hands and the fingers remain relaxed. There is a very subtle energy in the index fingers. The wrists are straight and relaxed so the life force can move more easily to the palms. The elbows point down, not to the sides. The distance between the arms is shoulder width: avoid having too wide or too narrow a space between the arms.

The arms are raised mainly by internal power generated at the scapulae. The height of the raised arms does not exceed the height of the shoulders.

Two-Hand Push

1. When the height of the arms reaches just below shoulder level, exhale slowly as you bend the elbows and sink the wrists so the palms face outward. This is accomplished by sinking the chest and shoulders.
2. Tilt the sacrum and sink the coccyx until you feel the nine points of the feet press firmly into the ground. Feel the earth force flow up the legs and spine.

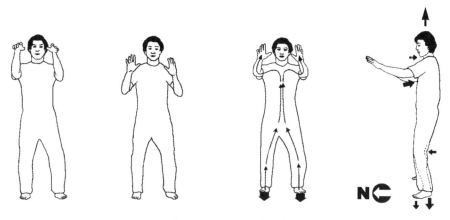

Fig. 5.6 Two-Hand Push

3. Round the scapulae, tilt the sacrum sightly inward, extend the arms, slightly sink the chest, and pull in the chin. Take care that the elbows remain slightly bent and the shoulders are not raised. Feel the upward force straighten the spine.

Lower the Arms

1. The arms are lowered through internal chi power. Relax the scapulae and tendon power holding the arms up. The wrists are relaxed and the hands return to the horizontal. The elbows remain bent, leading the movement

downward, as if the wrists were suspended by strings. The arms should feel as if they are floating or moving in water.

2. The hands come down as far as the level of the hips, and the next movement begins.

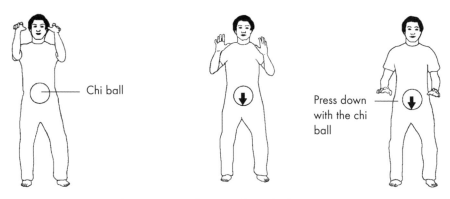

Chi ball

Press down with the chi ball

Fig. 5.7 Lower the arms through chi pressure

CORE MOVEMENTS: LEFT-HAND FORM

The next sequence is the core of the Tai Chi form; it is repeated in the four directions. These movements begin with the Left-Hand Form and then go through a transition into the Right-Hand Form. At the end there is a series of concluding movements.

The first half of Tai Chi Chi Kung is called the Left-Hand Form. The moves progress counterclockwise.

Grasping the Bird's Tail: North

First Ward Off: Holding the Chi Ball

1. Begin to inhale and relax as you sink most of your weight into the right leg. Allow the life force in the tan tien to lead the rotation to the left (west). Avoid the mistake of turning the head and shoulders first. As the waist and hips turn left, simply lift the left toes and allow the left foot to pivot on the heel.

2. As the waist turns, the left hand swings in a counterclockwise circle to about the height of the heart. The elbow points down. The right hand turns palm up, as if scooping, and swings to just below the navel. The wrists and fingers in both hands are straight yet relaxed. The distance the arms are held from the body is determined by the sinking of the chest and

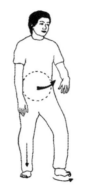

Fig. 5.8 First Ward Off: Holding the Chi Ball

rounding of the scapulae. The best measure is the position of the arms in Embracing the Tree—see page 229. (If the wrist of the left arm was turned so the palm faces in, it would be positioned exactly at the height and distance from the body as in Iron Shirt.) As the rotation is completed, the toes of the left foot are put down pointing west.

3. As you exhale, begin to shift about 60 percent of the body's weight to the left foot. The central line of gravity running from the crown through the perineum is aligned with the left foot. This allows you to balance your structure for the next movement. If the central line of gravity is not over the left foot, the next movement will be unbalanced and off-center.

Second Ward Off: Rolling the Chi Ball

1. As you inhale, your mind moves the tan tien energy to the right. The hips follow. The upper structure moves until the hips face northwest. At the same time, shift 100 percent of the balance to the left foot and lift the right heel. Keep the right toes touching the ground until you feel totally poised on the left leg and until the right leg feels it can effortlessly float off the ground without disturbing your balance.

2. Sink slightly lower into the left leg as you step out wide to the north with the right foot, which is free of weight. The length of the step is determined by the length of your leg and how far it can reach without losing the central line of gravity. Place the right foot so that the two feet are shoulder-width apart.

3. After the right heel touches the ground, begin to exhale as the rest of the foot comes down with the toes pointing directly forward (north). Transfer about 50 percent of the weight to the right foot. Simultaneous to transferring the weight, the right arm comes up from below to the height of the heart, the palm facing toward the chest. The height, position, and angle

Fig. 5.9 Second Ward Off: Rolling the Chi Ball

of the arm are exactly the same as in Embracing the Tree. The left elbow is dropped just a little so that the left palm faces toward the right palm, the fingers pointing up. The right hand holds the energy ball (now about the size of a medium cantaloupe) from the front and the left hand holds it from the back. Keep the chest sunk. The center of gravity is now distributed equally over both feet. You are now facing northwest, with the left foot pointing west and the right foot pointing north.

4. Keeping the tailbone dropped, begin to inhale as you shift the weight on the left to the inner heel and rotate the left leg inward. The left foot turns 45 degrees to the northwest, pressing the ground.

5. Direct the tan tien force to turn to the right. As the hips begin to turn to face north, the right knee is turning outward toward the right. This creates a spiraling, screwing motion that keeps the legs rooted to the ground. As the left foot begins to turn outward a spiraling motion is created, which begins to transfer the energy up the leg.

6. As the hips turn to face the front, tilt the sacrum inward until you feel a solid connection to the ground. In addition to pressing down and spiraling, the left leg begins to push forward. This push of the leg allows the spiraling energy to transfer upward to the hip and the spine.

As the left leg pushes forward, exhale and shift forward until the weight is about 70 percent on the right foot. The arms remain in position until the left foot is finished spiraling and pushing forward. The hips face north. The spiraling energy is propelled upward by the movements of the sacral and T11 pumps. As soon as the energy reaches C7, sink the chest and round the scapulae. The elbows remain slightly bent. The spiraling force is transferred from the scapulae to C7 and out through the arms to the hands.

Simultaneous with the sinking of the chest, the chin moves slightly to the back in a recoiling motion. This move adds the energy of the cranial pump and prevents the discharge of energy through the hands from whip-lashing the neck. It also keeps the central line of gravity aligned with the perineum and the right leg.

Take care that the right knee does not extend out over the right toes and that the torso is not leaning forward, breaking the central line of gravity. Relax everything.

Rollback

1. Begin inhaling and feel the earth force pulling the sacrum down as you sink slightly deeper into the right leg. The heavenly force produces a corresponding counter-pull up. The right leg then begins to push into the earth and the left knee bends, moving the structure back. The feet remain exactly where they are. Straighten the right wrist and extend the fingers to point forward so the palm no longer faces the body but instead faces the left side. The left arm rotates the hand so the palm faces up. As you sink back, bring the left hand under the right hand and pass it along the underside of the right arm (but without touching the right arm) until it is just under the right elbow.

   Take care to keep the chest sunk and the arms rounded. Don't allow the right arm to collapse so it moves closer to the body.

2. Exhale as your mind directs your tan tien chi to turn to the left. The hips turn slightly to the right as your tan tien and waist turn left, creating a slight torque. The upper structure of the spine and arms remain exactly as they are. As you turn, extend the spiraling into the right arm so the right hand rotates until the palm is turned toward the face.

   The most common mistake in rolling back is turning the head and eyes first, followed by the shoulders and finally the hips. Turning the head and shoulders first twists the spine, compromising the strength of your structure.

Press down
with the chi
ball

Move the
chi ball left

Fig. 5.10 Rollback

Two-Hand Press

1. When the turn to the left reaches about 60 percent of your limit, begin the left arm movement without twisting the spine. Inhale as the left arm describes a scooping circle with the palm up. The hand never goes above the level of the ear.

2. As the left hand describes the upper part of the circle, the tan tien chi starts to direct the hips to turn back toward the north. These two moves are synchronized so that the heel of the left hand completes the circle and comes to press on the heel of the right hand at the same instant that the hips complete their turn to the north. The left hand supports the right wrist, reducing the potential for injury when pushing forcefully into an opponent.

3. Most of the weight is on the left foot throughout the previous moves. Once the hands meet and the hips face north, begin to spiral and transfer the energy forward to discharge it through the hands.

   A common mistake is to begin transferring the weight to the right foot before aligning the hips to face directly forward. The spiraling energy is then dissipated before it reaches the hands, and the move is totally ineffective.

   The spiraling of the energy begins as you exhale and press the left foot

*Tai Chi Chi
Kung Thirteen
Movement Form*

Fig. 5.11 Two-Hand Press

to the ground. The left knee turns outward to the left side. As the left leg begins to push forward, the right knee spirals outward to the right. When the spiraling energy reaches the sacrum, align and activate the sacral pump by tucking slightly in. As the left leg push continues and the spiraling energy reaches T11, add the force of the T11 pump by curving and pushing a little at T11. Eventually the force will reach C7; the pump at C7 is activated by sinking the chest and rounding the scapulae.

4. As the force is transferred through the arms and begins to reach the hands, the right hand twists clockwise while the left hand twists counterclockwise, as when you open a jar. The last movement is pulling the chin back to activate the cranial pump.

   About 70 percent of the weight is now on the right foot. Take care that the right knee is not extended beyond the right toes.

Two-Hand Push

1. Inhale, relax, and sink back on the left foot. The sacrum is pulled down once again and the heavenly pull stretches the spine up. The right leg in front begins to push into the earth, moving the structure back. Take care not to bounce up; the body moves level to the ground.

2. Maintaining their connection, both hands turn palms down. Start to separate the hands by drawing the left hand lightly over the top of the right hand.

3. Continue to separate the hands until they are shoulder-width apart. Sink the elbows while keeping the hands in line with the forearms, bringing the palms to face the front. The shape and position of the hand relative to the forearm in this movement and throughout the form is referred to as Fair Lady's Hand. Fair Lady's Hand is a perfect blending of yin and yang: the fingers are straight but not too straight, relaxed but not collapsed, separated but not too far apart. The wrists are bent neither forward nor backward, a position that could be described as regal or elegant. Although it looks as if the elbows are contracting and coming closer to the chest, this is not the case. The chest remains sunk and the scapulae rounded. The correct height of the hands is approximately level with the ears. This is also called Protecting the Head.

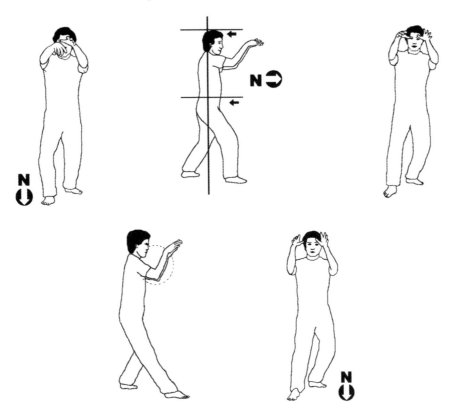

Fig. 5.12 Sink back

4. After sinking back, the next move is pushing forward. Once again, begin to exhale as the left leg presses down into the earth. As the energy spirals

upward, activate the sacral, T11, and C7 pumps. Feel as though the body is going to jump upward, but take care not to bounce.

As the energy reaches C7 and spreads to the arms, refrain from pushing from the elbows. Let the energy from the scapulae provide the main force. Add the energy of the cranial pump toward the end of the move by pushing the chin back.

5. When the energy reaches the palms and spreads to the fingers, the tendon power stretches the fingers but the centers of the palms remain relaxed. Take care that the center of the palms does not reach outward so that the fingers bend back; the wrists remain perfectly straight in alignment with the forearms. A common mistake is bending the wrists backward. In a combat situation, such a position is vulnerable and could lead to wrist injury by allowing an opponent to bend your hands backward. Instead, twist the left arm and hand clockwise and spiral the right arm and hand counterclockwise.

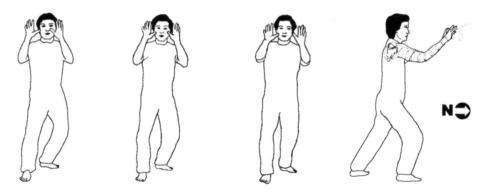

Fig. 5.13 Two-Hand Push

🌀 Single Whip: South

First Twist: Shift and Pivot

1. Inhale as you sink back into the left leg. The elbows straighten, but not completely; always keep a slight bend in the elbows and knees to allow the chi to flow through the joints. The palms face down toward the ground, with the arms parallel to the ground.

2. Begin to exhale as your mind directs the tan tien chi to turn to the left. The hips follow the turning of the chi. The spine, shoulders, and head are turned by the turning of the hips; they do not turn independently.

3. During the turning of the hips, allow the right leg and foot, which are in front, to be pulled along and turned by the hips. Simply lift the right toes

Fig. 5.14 Single Whip: sink back

and pivot the foot on the heel. Continue turning until the hips cannot turn any more (the hips will turn about 90 degrees to face the west). The right foot pivots, toes pointing west, then the sole is put back on the ground. It's important to keep the left leg stable as you turn the hips. Allow the left hip joint to rotate and close as much as possible as you turn.

4. Then release the lower back and turn the waist independent of the hips, twisting the lumbar vertebrae until the arms face southwest. Exert a slight countertwist to the right with the hips to keep them stationary as the waist and upper body twist to the left. Continue the twist with the upper spine and shoulders until the arms face south. A common mistake is to keep turning the head, eyes, and shoulders after the hips have ceased to turn, thus twisting the spine.

Turning the waist produces a coiling force in the left leg, like a rubber band coiled around a stick in one direction. If the rubber band is attached to the end of that stick, when the stick is released it spins as the energy releases from the coil of the rubber band. Think of the left leg as the rubber band and the arms as the stick at the end. The movement winds up the force in the leg and releases it up the leg, through the spine, and out the arms.

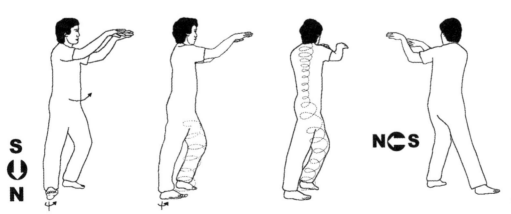

Tai Chi Chi
Kung Thirteen
Movement Form

Fig. 5.15 Single Whip: shift

Second Twist: Forming the Beak

1. When you've reached your maximum turn to the left, inhale as you press the left leg to the ground and shift to the right. As you shift, allow the elbows to bend slightly.

2. Once you have shifted your weight to the right, exhale as the hips turn toward the right. The coiled energy in the left leg is thus transferred to the right leg. All the weight is now on the right leg.

Fig. 5.16 Single Whip: Forming the Beak

3. As the hips are turning right, the right arm bends at the elbow and the right hand forms into a beak. The thumb and the pinkie finger touch, and all the other fingers press around them. The beak is an offensive weapon for pecking forcefully or for grabbing. If the little finger is not protected by the other fingers, it can easily be broken.

4. Simultaneously, as the right arm contracts and forms the beak, the left hand comes under the right elbow in a scooping motion. A common mistake is moving the right arm tightly close to the body and bringing the left arm to almost touch the abdomen. The sinking of the chest and the

Fig. 5.17 Single Whip: striking the beak

circularity of the arms is lost. The transfer of the force coiled in the leg then is broken at the scapulae.

The wrist of the right (beak) hand is held at a height between the shoulder and the bottom of the ear.

Third Twist: Releasing the Beak

1. Inhale and begin releasing the coiled energy in the right leg by directing the tan tien chi to turn the hip to the left. As the energy is released and the hip is turned left, the left foot pivots on the big toe. All the weight remains poised on the right leg.

2. As the force uncoils, it travels up the spine and is released through the right arm and the beak. The beak is extended to the west, keeping the elbow slightly bent at the end of the movement. If the elbow was completely straightened or locked, it would be very difficult to retract the arm if it was grabbed, and the elbow could easily be dislocated.

Fig. 5.18 Single Whip: Releasing the Beak

Reaching to Heaven

1. Once the coiled energy has been released through the right arm and all the weight is on the right foot, the left leg is free to step out wide. The central line of gravity running from crown through perineum should be positioned directly over the right foot, so that you are completely balanced on the right leg and the step with the left leg is smooth. If not, the step has to be made quickly before you fall. The left foot aims for an angle 45 degrees to the left from where the right foot is positioned. Once again, if you are working inside, the leg faces toward the corner of the room while the foot faces the wall. The heel of the left foot touches the ground first. The feet, if viewed from above, are at a 90-degree angle to each other. The right foot is still pointing to the west and the left foot to the south.

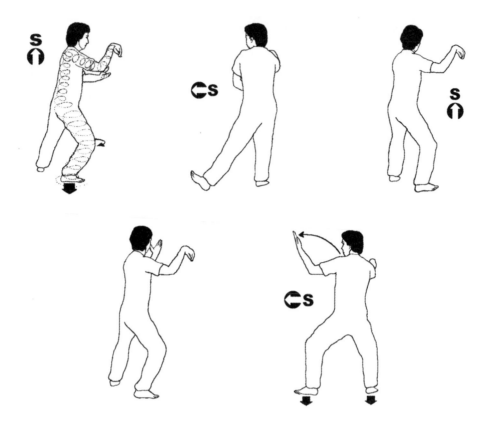

Fig. 5.19 Single Whip: blocking with the hand

2. Exhale as the weight is shifted so it is equally distributed between the two feet.

   Simultaneous to the shifting, the toes of the left foot come down, pointing directly south, bringing the other eight points of the foot into firm contact with the ground.

3. At the same time as you make this shift, the left arm describes an arc with the palm facing the body; the left hand rises to the height of the face, about a forearm's length away from the face. Make certain to keep both shoulders relaxed and both elbows pointing toward the ground. The left hand opens palm upward (reaching toward heaven), and the right hand retains the beak.

   When the weight is equal on both feet, the right arm is positioned over the right leg and the left arm is over the left leg. The groin is open; the hips face southwest.

Single-Hand Push

1. Inhale and turn the right foot to face 45 degrees toward the southwest, pivoting on the heel. The mind then directs the tan tien chi to turn left. The hips follow.

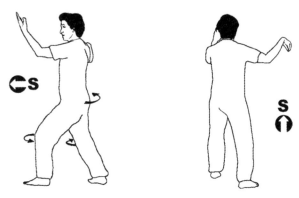

Fig. 5.20 Single Whip: rooting

2. Exhale as the right foot presses into the ground and begins to spiral the energy up the right leg.

3. The right leg begins to push into the ground, moving the hip to face south and spiraling the energy up into the hips and spine. The sacral, T11, and C7 pumps are activated as the energy spirals up. The chest is sunk and the scapulae rounded, transferring the force out the left arm. Finally, the force of the cranial pump is added by moving the chin back in a recoil action. The elbow of the left arm is kept slightly bent, so the wrist of the left hand is not bent. Make sure the weight is 70 percent in the front leg. Open the groin of the front leg and let your connection to the ground be strong down the inside of the front leg.

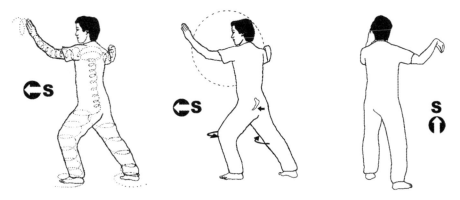

Fig. 5.21 Single Whip: Single-Hand Push

After completing the above sections, two more repetitions of Grasping the Bird's Tail and Single Whip are performed, ending with a Single Whip to the north.

Grasping the Bird's Tail: West

Transition Movement: Sink Back to Protect the Chest

1. Inhale and sink down on the right leg. At the same time, rotate the left wrist so the palm faces the body. The proper measure for this move is the Embracing the Tree arm position.

2. Simultaneously, the right arm comes down to the side near the thigh, relaxing the fingers. The chest remains sunk and the scapulae rounded.

Fig. 5.22 Transition Movement: Sink Back

First Ward Off: Holding the Chi Ball

1. Exhale and push forward with the right leg until the weight is about 60 percent on the left leg. The left hand begins to turn, palm facing down. The right hand comes scooping from below.

2. Simultaneously, the tan tien chi moves left, turning the hips. Take care that the hips turn the spine, shoulders, and head.

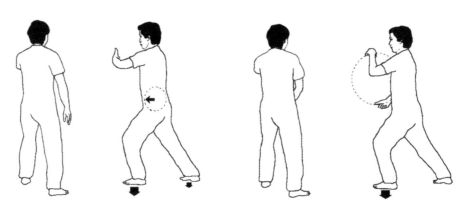

Fig. 5.23 Forming the chi ball

Second Ward Off: Rolling the Chi Ball

From here the set repeats itself exactly as before but with a new directional orientation. The rest of Grasping the Bird's Tail is now performed facing the west, followed by Single Whip to the east.

Rollback

Fig. 5.24a First half of Second Ward Off

Two-Hand Press

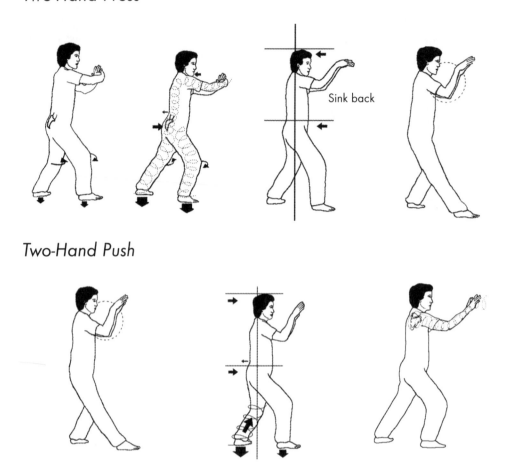

Sink back

Two-Hand Push

Fig. 5.24b Remainder of movements for Second Ward Off

⟳ Single Whip: East

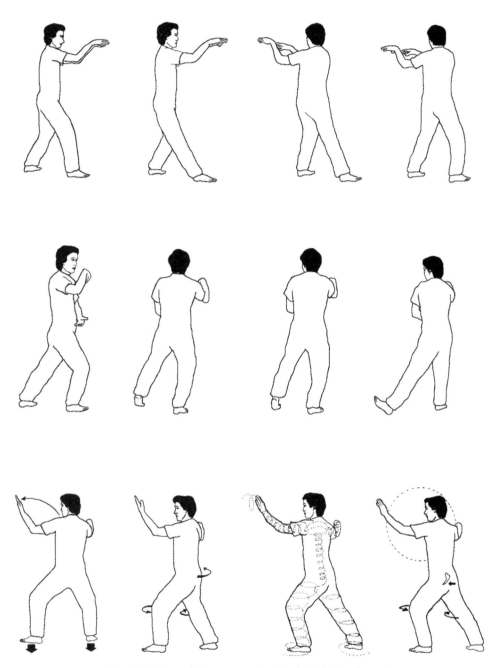

Fig. 5.25 Complete movements: Single Whip to the east

Grasping the Bird's Tail: South

Do another repetition of the core movements; this time perform Grasping the Bird's Tail to the south, followed by Single Whip to the north.

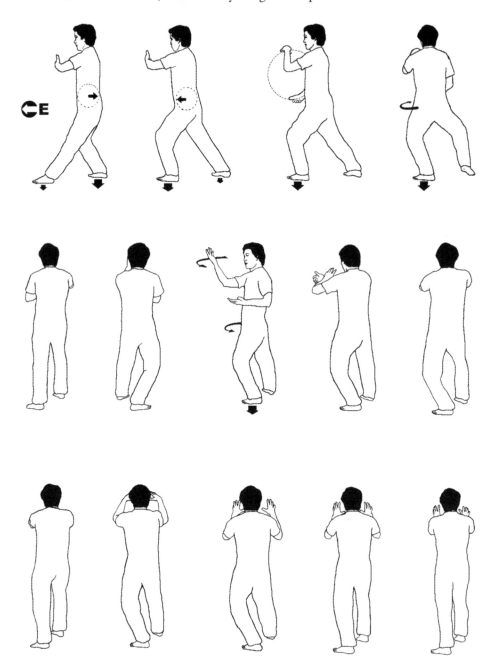

Fig. 5.26 Complete movements: Grasping the Bird's Tail to the south

Single Whip: North

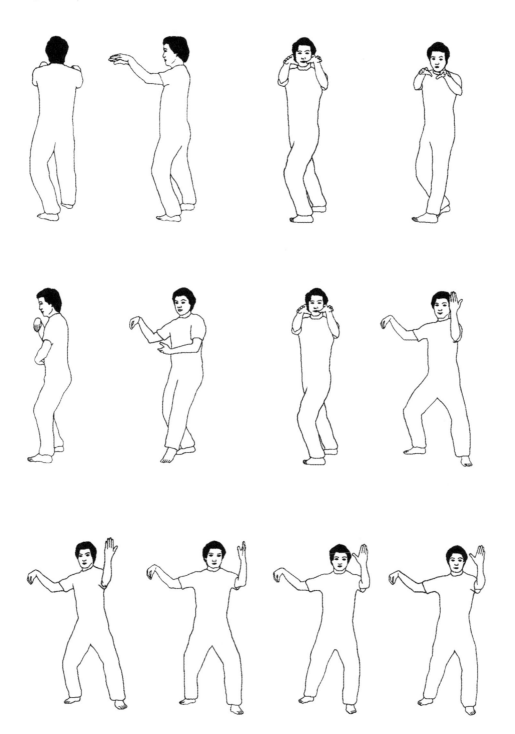

Fig. 5.27 Complete movements: Single Whip to the north

CORE MOVEMENTS: RIGHT-HAND FORM

Up to this point, all movements have been done turning to the left side. With the transition, all the movements are done turning to the right side.

⚙ Transition to Right-Hand Form: Holding the Baby

1. The left and right arms drop as the tan tien chi turns the hips to the right (northeast). Both palms turn up.
2. Feel the chi pressure in the tan tien.

Fig. 5.28 Transition

⚙ Grasping the Bird's Tail: North

First Ward Off

In this transition movement into the Right-Hand Form there is no First Ward Off movement. In all subsequent repetitions of Grasping the Bird's Tail you perform First Ward Off as in the Left-Hand Form, but with left and right hands and feet reversed.

Second Ward Off

1. The right arm describes a circle, not going above the level of the right ear. The left arm comes up to the position of Ward Off. At the same time the weight shifts to the left leg, which is in the front. The hips turn to face forward as the arm movement is completed.

2. The palms are holding an energy ball in front. The position is the Second Ward Off. This set continues exactly as outlined for the Left-Hand Form, but with opposite hands.

Fig. 5.29 Second Ward Off: Right-Hand Form

Rollback

Fig. 5.30 Rollback: Right-Hand Form

Press

Fig. 5.31 Press: Right-Hand Form

Push

Fig. 5.32 Push: Right-Hand Form

◉ Single Whip: South

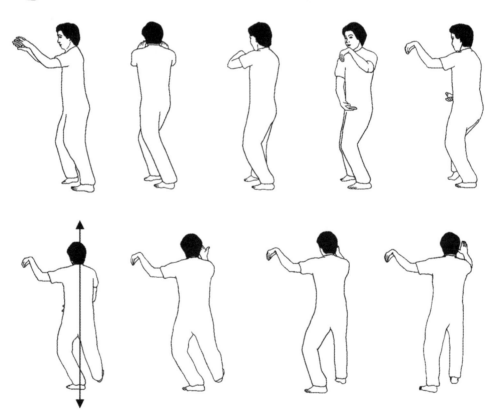

Fig. 5.33 Single Whip: Right-Hand Form

Grasping the Bird's Tail: East

Sink Back to Protect Chest

Fig. 5.34 Sink Back

First Ward Off

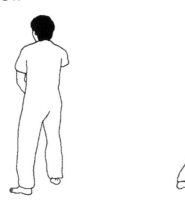

Fig. 5.35 First Ward Off: Holding the Chi Ball

Second Ward Off

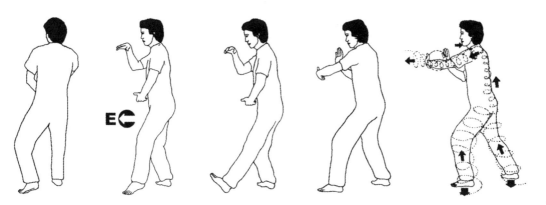

Fig. 5.36 Second Ward Off

Tai Chi Chi Kung Thirteen Movement Form

Rollback

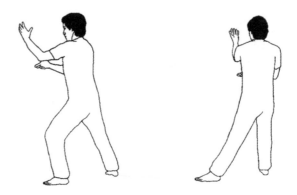

Fig. 5.37 Rollback

Press

Fig. 5.38 Press

Sink Back

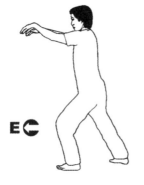

Fig. 5.39 Sink Back

⟳ Single Whip: West

Fig. 5.40 Single Whip to the west

⬡ Grasping the Bird's Tail: South

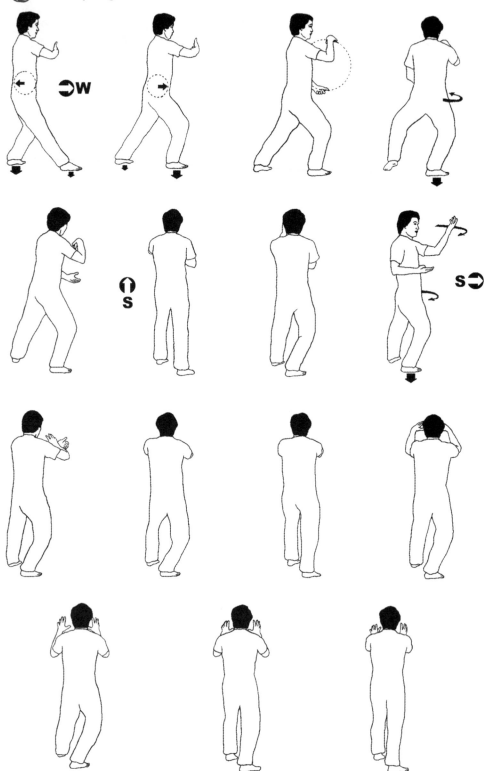

Fig. 5.41 Grasping the Bird's Tail to the south

Single Whip: North

Fig. 5.42 Single Whip to the north

CONCLUDING MOVEMENTS

The concluding movements close the Tai Chi form. After you have generated and absorbed all the surrounding energy, it is important to collect the energy in the tan tien for storage.

🌀 Cross Hands

1. Inhale as you shift the weight back to the left leg. At the same time, raise the hands above the head and in front of the body so the palms face out and up, with the fingers pointing toward each other.
2. Circle the arms out to the sides. As they pass shoulder level, exhale as you raise the right toes, step straight back with the right leg, and touch the toes down shoulder width from the left foot, with the right foot facing north.
3. The two hands continue to scoop down in a large circular motion to the sides. At the same time, shift all the weight to the right leg.
4. Inhale and continue scooping the arms inward until the wrists cross in front of the navel with the palms facing up, collecting all the surrounding

Fig. 5.43 Closing of Tai Chi Chi Kung I

energy through the arms and into the navel. Simultaneously step in with the left leg and place the left foot next to the right foot. The knees should still be bent.

5. Shift the weight to the middle so it is equally divided between the two legs. The hands, still crossed at the wrists, continue rising in front of the body until they reach throat level.

⟳ Closing Tai Chi: Hun Yuan Stance

1. Separate the two hands, palms up, to shoulder-width apart.
2. Then begin to exhale as you turn the palms to face downward and slowly lower the arms.
3. As the hands approach waist level the legs slowly straighten, returning to full standing height.
4. Finally, bring the arms back to the sides in the same position as at the beginning of the form, in Wu Chi stance.
5. Stand for a minute, breathing naturally. Feel the energy you have generated through performing Tai Chi Chi Kung. Let all the channels open and just allow the energy to flow freely though the entire body. Feel that there is one connected river of chi in the body, with no obstructions or blockages anywhere. Take time to enjoy this sensation with full awareness.

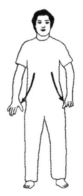

Fig. 5.44 Closing stance

⟲ Collecting Energy

At the end, as with all the practices of the Tao, collect the energy by placing both hands over the navel. If you are a man, use your mental forces to spiral the energy thirty-six times in a clockwise direction followed by twenty-four times in a counterclockwise direction; if you are a woman, spiral thirty-six times counterclockwise and twenty-four times clockwise. If you want, you may shorten the collecting by spiraling nine times in each direction.

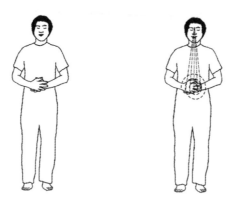

Fig. 5.45 Collecting the energy at the navel

SUMMARY: COMPONENTS OF THE TAI CHI CHI KUNG FORM

Use the following outline of the Tai Chi Chi Kung movements to help you learn the names of the different movements and remember the sequence.

Introductory Movements

Wu Chi Stance

Smile

Breathe in Energy

Opening Tai Chi

Preparation: Step Out

Raise the Arms

Two-Hand Push

Lower the Arms

Core Movements: Left-Hand Form

Grasping the Bird's Tail: North

First Ward Off: Holding the Chi Ball

Second Ward Off: Rolling the Chi Ball

Rollback

*Tai Chi Chi
Kung Thirteen
Movement Form*

6

Sequence for Home Practice

The sequence for home practice is divided into three levels: beginning, intermediate, and advanced. Having a solid foundation in the beginning stages ensures better understanding of the intermediate and advanced levels.

BEGINNING LEVEL

As stated earlier, Tai Chi Chi Kung is a continuation of various meditation practices, including the Inner Smile, Microcosmic Orbit meditation, and the Fusion practice. It is important to support Tai Chi with regular meditation practice. Tai Chi is also a continuation of Iron Shirt Chi Kung, so it is vital to practice the different positions of Iron Shirt, especially Embracing the Tree and Golden Turtle Submerging in Water.

Wu Chi Stance

Dedicate some time to practicing the first position of Tai Chi, known as the Wu Chi stance. This requires simply standing still and allowing the body to relax as much as possible. Standing in this position, make sure there is no leaning in any direction. The heavenly pull is the best guide for this. The moment you lean, the pull from above is decreased or cut off. Experiment with this; your experience will tune you in to the best structural connection.

Stand still for several minutes, allowing the body to relax as much as possible in the posture. Any pain that begins to develop in any area is an excellent indication of misalignments in the Wu Chi stance.

nine points of the feet touching the ground and
weight is equally distributed on both feet. Make sure
are not contracted as though they are gripping the

...ess to your knees. Check to see that the knees are
that the weight of the body does not jam up in the
...es were hyperextended backward, as though locked
...s puts too much of the load-bearing work onto the
...ack and cuts off the chi and blood circulation from

...your feet from the heels to the soles, gradually feel
...your feet and away from your knees. Your weight
...r on your heel, sending the force down the back of
...front.

...r awareness up your legs to your back and check that
...e area of the lumbar vertebrae due to a tilted pelvis.
...s not slumped forward.
...our awareness up your back to your shoulders. Check
...not tense or raised upward. Continue directing your
...he base of the skull and make sure the chin is slightly
...a feeling of openness through the back of the neck.

...ur head is not leaning forward. Feel a slight pull upward
...heavenly force draws the earth force upward. Relax as
...t the heavenly pull hold you suspended and stretch the

...o adjust the angle of the head. Move very slowly. Notice
...flows from the soles of the feet to the crown when the
...ong.

...yes open and relaxed. Focus your vision directly ahead, not
...sky. Then become aware of the corners of your eyes being
...ubtle inner smile.

...aws and make sure they are not closed tightly. The back
...t be pressing down hard. Keep the tongue lightly touching
...mfortable angle that does not produce a lot of saliva.

Corners of the mouth. The corners of the mouth are slightly raised by an inner smile. Relax the muscles of the neck and throat as much as possible. Swallowing a little saliva helps relax the muscles.

Chest. Move your awareness to your sternum. If there is tension at the sternum, inhale slowly without straining further and slowly exhale through the mouth until there is no more air in the lungs.

Lower abdomen. Check that the muscles of the lower abdomen are relaxed, naturally and effortlessly expanding with each inhalation and contracting with each exhalation.

Anus and perineum. Place your attention at the anus and create a very subtle contraction. It is important that this anal contraction not be forceful, as that would generate strain throughout the torso. The contraction is, rather, the result of good muscular tone in the perineum. Maintain this subtle contraction throughout your practice.

Armpits. Bring your awareness to your armpits. Leave enough space under the armpits for each to hold a Ping-Pong ball.

Palms. Allow the center of the palms to be fully relaxed and let the fingers hang freely.

While doing the complete Tai Chi Chi Kung set, pay attention to each of the following points.

Points to Observe

The center of gravity is mainly centered on the tan tien.
The heavenly pull is always maintained.
The speed is even throughout.
The movements flow continuously without jerks or sudden changes.
The breath is even and never held.
Natural abdominal breathing is maintained throughout.
The chest is lightly sunk and the scapulae rounded.
The nine points of the feet always touch the ground fully when you are not
   stepping.
Yin and yang, fullness and emptiness, are distinguished in each step.
The hips guide the movements of the torso.
The structure of the back is not broken when sinking down.
The elbows always point to the ground.

During each round of practice, select one of the points above for special emphasis. Stay with that point until you feel you have it mastered, and then select a different point for emphasis.

Holding the Position

Begin the Tai Chi set. Stop on each position and hold it while you check the following.

Is there a pull at the crown?

Is the spine aligned?

Is there any leaning?

Is the center of gravity around the lower abdomen?

Do the knees extend beyond the edge of the toes?

Are the nine points of the feet making contact with the ground?

Is the position solid or unstable?

Are the eyes looking ahead?

Is the breathing relaxed?

Take your time with each posture. Gradually increase the length of time you hold each posture, starting at thirty seconds and building up to five minutes. Watch for developing pains and strains; they may give you an indication of subtle misalignments.

INTERMEDIATE LEVEL

When all the points covered in the beginning level have been integrated into the Tai Chi form, you can continue the refining process at the intermediate level.

Feel the muscles separating from the bones. Experience deep relaxation in the meditation practice to the point where you feel the muscles separating from the bones. This level of relaxation allows a far more efficient flow of life force than anything previously experienced. Bring that level of relaxation into the movements of Tai Chi.

Guide the form with the mind/eye/heart and chi flow. As a continuation of moving in deep relaxation, allow the Tai Chi movements to be guided primarily by the mind and chi and less by the muscular contraction that is typically used in the beginning level.

Maintain a smooth and even tempo. Observe the rate at which the movements are done at the beginning of the set and aim at having that same flow in the last movements of the set. Since the emphasis here is on the gracefulness of your Tai Chi, the rate must be uniform throughout your practice.

Concentrate on energy discharge. Begin by separating each element of the movement and feel the energy being transferred at each stage. Practicing with slow movements, you are able to feel the exact position of the energy at each stage.

Regulate the size of the step. The best guide is marking the spot where you begin the set. If the steps are always equal, you will finish the set on the same spot at which the form began or very near to it. Even steps also place you facing the exact direction of each transition.

Regulating the measure of your step depends on the length of your legs. When the step is too short, the practitioner usually ends up with the knees extending over the edge of the toes, which puts too much weight on the knees and causes knee pain. If the step is too wide, the center of gravity is lost.

Check for leaning. The specific signs are one shoulder is higher than the other; the hands are not equal when pushing or turning; the hip bone and sacrum are tilted to one side when sinking back; you lean forward during Push and Ward Off; you lean back during sinking motions.

ADVANCED PRACTICE

When all the points covered in the beginning and intermediate levels have been assimilated into the form without having to think or check each item, you are considered to have reached an advanced level of Tai Chi practice. Here are the important points to follow at this level.

1. The calmness of mind cultivated through meditation leads to an absence of random thoughts. Aim at maintaining that state during Tai Chi.
2. Sense the energy flow at each stage of the movements. Let the mind dissolve into energy and movement.
3. Maintain even breathing throughout. Inhale during the yin phase of each movement (sinking back, turning, etc.); exhale during the yang phase (Ward Off, Push, Single Whip, etc.). Eventually the coordinated inhalations and exhalations should happen automatically and without conscious effort.
4. Keep your gaze steady without excessive blinking or looking around. The eyes are the mirror of the mind and the spirit. Keep your eyes relaxed yet alert.

5. Maintain total concentration on the movements without being disturbed by sounds.
6. Acquire muscular relaxation and suppleness, yet be ready to discharge energy instantly.
7. Move and step noiselessly.
8. Remain centered at the tan tien throughout the set.

Yin/Yang and Inner Smile Form

YIN AND YANG IN TAI CHI CHI KUNG

The inseparability, interpenetration, and dynamism of yin and yang are expressed by the Tai Chi symbol. The Tai Chi symbol represents movement: the yang pushing the yin and the yin drawing in the yang. The original Chinese characters for yin and yang depicted the dark and sunny sides of a mountain. Their qualities are relative; the yang side is hot, bright, and dry in contrast to the yin side, which is cold, dark, and wet.

Fig. 7.1 Yin and yang symbol

As profound as it may be, this symbol is no more than a symbol; the concept of yin and yang is without value unless it can be related to the continuous movement of the dance of life.

The changes of yin and yang maintain the circle of balance in nature; night follows day, the moon follows the sun, winter follows summer. When the winter gets too cold, we know the warmer spring is coming. When the summer gets too hot, we know the cool autumn weather is near.

Similarly, in Tai Chi Chi Kung the concept of yin and yang is given physical reality. Tai Chi is a way of experiencing yin and yang consciously. Certain movements are more characteristically yin while others are more yang. Specific physical interpretations of yin and yang are shown in the following table.

Yin	Yang
Earth	Heaven
Inhaling	Exhaling
Drawing in energy	Discharging energy
Sinking down	Rising up
Retreating	Advancing
Closing	Opening
Lowering	Raising
Bending	Straightening
Contracting	Expanding
Receptive	Active
Supportive	Dominant
Yielding	Firm
Bottom	Top
Storing	Releasing
Inner	Outer
Soft	Hard
Defense	Attack

As indicated by the Tai Chi symbol, every movement in Tai Chi Chi Kung is a particular combination of yin and yang: the more yang, the less yin; the more yin, the less yang. The sequence of movements in Tai Chi is choreographed such that the relative proportions of yin and yang are constantly changing. A situation that could be initially characterized as primarily yin transforms itself, through the flow of the movements, into a situation that could be described as primarily yang by gradually increasing the yang and correspondingly decreasing the yin.

Although the proportions of yin and yang are constantly changing, we conventionally describe the movements in terms of the pole we are moving toward. Hence the changes described in the previous sentence would be expressed thus: greatest yin to lesser yin to lesser yang to greatest yang to lesser yang to lesser yin to greatest yin. This cycle continues to repeat itself throughout the Tai Chi Chi Kung form.

RELAXATION AND ACTIVITY

Relaxation is the key to being able to distinguish yin from yang and vice versa. Relaxation is the foundation of activity. It is also crucial to absorbing chi. Smiling, as taught in the practice of the Inner Smile, is an extremely effective relaxation technique. It is important to begin the Tai Chi Chi Kung form with a smile and to smile continuously throughout your practice.

The smile I'm speaking of begins in the eyes and spreads across the face, slightly lifting the corners of the mouth. The smile is then directed to the organs, particularly the heart and kidneys. Smiling to the joints helps them to open, resulting in freer movement. Smiling to the muscles relaxes them, separating them from the bones, which results in smoother chi flow. Smiling to the bones draws energy into them. The goal of Tai Chi Chi Kung is to use the mind to absorb, transform, and direct chi. The Inner Smile sets the stage for accomplishing this goal.

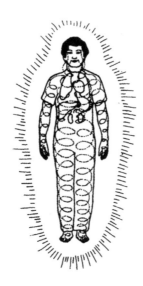

Fig. 7.2 The Inner Smile sets the stage for absorbing, transforming, and directing chi

EARTH AND HEAVEN

It is helpful to use the image of the tree in beginning the Tai Chi Chi Kung form, as it depicts an ideal arrangement for absorbing energy. The roots are sunk deep in the ground, absorbing the earth force; the trunk reaches up to absorb the heavenly force; the leaves spread out to absorb the cosmic force.

To initiate the Tai Chi Chi Kung form, lightly tuck in the sacrum so the coccyx aligns with the spine and the force is felt at the lumbar region. This

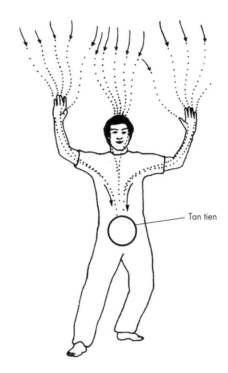

Fig. 7.3 Absorbing the earth force   **Fig. 7.4** Absorbing the heavenly force

subtle movement presses the nine points of the feet more firmly into the ground. Lightly and gradually rock the feet from the soles to the heels, until you feel the force move up the heels to the hips and spine. Feel Bubbling Springs, the Kidney 1 point on the soles of the feet, activate as the earth energy draws up into the feet and then travels up the legs and into the spine at the coccyx.

The earth energy initiates a wavelike motion in the spine. Once the energy reaches the scapulae, the chi causes the arms to rise to shoulder height. As the chest sinks and the chin is pulled in, the energy continues up through the cervical spine to the crown. As the crown, the highest part of the body, extends up, a connection is made with the heavenly force. An upward pull is experienced, so the whole skeletal frame feels as if it were suspended from above.

Throughout the form, maintain your connection with the three forces: earth force, heavenly force, and cosmic force. Feel rooted to the earth yet pulled toward the heavens. The fingers are spread, gently moving like leaves swaying in a breeze, as you feel the cosmic force. The cosmic force is experienced as an ocean of chi all around you.

Energy is drawn in during the yin phase of movement. The process of

Yin/Yang and Inner Smile Form

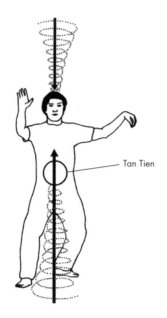

Fig. 7.5 Harmonizing the heaven and earth forces at the tan tien

Tan Tien

emptying, which is considered to be yin, creates more space to be filled. Breathing is an example of this dynamic. The end of an inhalation is fully yin on the outside of the body. At this point the lungs are fully yang on the inside—completely expanded. As the hot yang air is expelled, the outside of the body becomes more yang while the insides are emptied, becoming yin, with an increased potential to absorb air. Softly absorb energy into the palms and soles; absorb gently as if you were pulling a silken thread.

The earth force is cool and enters through the most yin part of the body: the feet; it is therefore considered yin. The heavenly force is hot and enters through the most yang part of the body: the head; it is therefore considered yang. Humanity exists between these two forces and is responsible for harmonizing them. As yin and yang energies are drawn in and combined and blended in the tan tien, they are transformed into a highly usable chi that can nourish the entire being as it is circulated in the Microcosmic Orbit.

EMPTINESS AND FULLNESS IN THE LEGS AND ARMS

One of the most important features of yin and yang in Tai Chi Chi Kung is the awareness of emptiness and fullness. Throughout the performance of the core movements, you shift weight back and forth between the right and left legs. The weight-bearing leg is the full leg; it is the more yang or active leg because it is doing the majority of the work in supporting the weight. Similarly, the empty leg is the one that is bearing little or none of the body's weight; it is more relaxed, more yin, empty of tension.

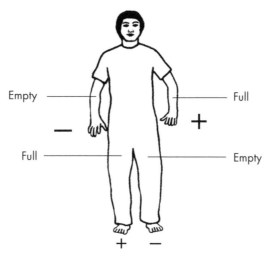

Fig. 7.6 Emptiness and fullness in the arms and legs

Keep in mind an important law of yin and yang: nothing is entirely yin or entirely yang. Yang always contains some yin and yin always has some yang in it. Therefore, *full* and *empty* refer to the predominant yin or yang quality of the leg. For example, the full leg is anywhere from 51 to 99 percent yang; yet, while yang may predominate, that leg is still anywhere from 1 to 49 percent yin.

Once you begin to move, you must clearly distinguish yin and yang. The full leg is the power leg, as it releases the stored energy, like a bow releasing an arrow. As you release the full leg it becomes empty and the empty leg, by being yin and receiving the body's weight as you shift, becomes yang, or full. The Tao Te Ching expresses this idea in the verses "That which would straighten must first be bent; that which would fill must first be empty."

The arms are always changing from empty to full in a similar way. One arm is always dominant and substantial while the other is supportive, receptive, and insubstantial. The full arm is always opposite the full leg. For example, when the weight is predominantly on the right leg, the left arm is the full arm.

FUNCTIONAL OPPOSITION

The full and empty sides change during each movement. For example, when executing the Push movement on the left-hand side, initially the right leg is forward and weighted. As you shift the weight back to the left leg, the right hand becomes the dominant hand and the left hand should be slightly more relaxed, playing a receptive and supportive role at first. As you begin to shift forward the right hand is dominant at the start of the push, but as the right leg begins to fill with the body's weight, the right hand should proportionately relax as the left hand becomes dominant.

This idea is illustrated in the way a right-handed baseball pitcher throws a ball. He first winds up and shifts his weight back into the right leg, storing energy. Then he shifts his weight forward into the left leg and releases the ball. Another example is in how you swing the arms when you walk or run. As one leg comes forward, the opposite arm swings forward as a counterbalance.

Functional opposition occurs throughout the Tai Chi Chi Kung form, serving to balance upper and lower, left and right. Functional opposition is a major technique for keeping yin and yang balanced in Tai Chi.

AVOID THE FAULT OF DOUBLE-WEIGHTEDNESS

Failing to distinguish clearly between yin and yang, emptiness and fullness, is called *double-weightedness*. Double-weightedness can happen in several ways. The first is when both arms try to be yang at the same time or when the weight falls evenly on both legs at the same time. (During the core movements, this is a fault; during the opening movements it is not a fault, as at that time you are expressing yin and yang in terms of up and down, expansion and contraction.) When the weight is divided 50–50 between the feet, it becomes more difficult to shift quickly to one side or the other. Many people have experienced this sensation in sports such as tennis and racquetball, when they were caught "flatfooted" and were unable to respond quickly.

The second way double-weightedness occurs is when both the upper and lower body on one side are both yang or both yin. To use the example of the baseball pitcher again, you never see a right-handed pitcher step forward with his right leg as he throws. Try this and you will see how awkward the movement is. To prevent this type of double-weightedness, always make sure that when you want power in your right arm, your weight shifts to the left leg and vice versa. Similarly, when you want the left arm to be yielding or empty, the right leg should also be empty. Following these rules of yin and yang will keep you in balance during your Tai Chi practice.

BENDING AND STRAIGHTENING

Bending is yin while straightening is yang. When we bend the arms, legs, and spine we are storing energy; when we straighten them we release that stored energy. The Tai Chi classics say, "Storing energy is like bending a bow; releasing energy is like shooting an arrow." For this reason, in Tai Chi the arms, legs, and spine are called the three bows. If you want to shoot the arrow a long distance, you must first bend the bow.

Beginners often neglect to bend the knees enough when shifting forward and back. This is why their movements lack power. Too much bending, however, can lead to collapse of one's structure, so it is important to bend neither too little nor too much.

Similarly, straightening the arms or legs too much can also lead to stiffness and overextending. In Chi Kung the joints are often referred to as the energy gates of the body. Thus, whenever you straighten the arms and legs you should never lock the knees and elbows; instead, always keep a slight flexion in these joints to keep the energy gates open. This allows the chi and blood to flow smoothly through the limbs without the obstruction you create when you lock the joints and inadvertently close the gates.

UP AND DOWN, ADVANCING AND RETREATING, LEFT AND RIGHT

The Tai Chi classics state: "If there is up, there is down; if there is retreating, there is advancing; if there is left, there is right. If your intention is to move up, you should at the same time contain the idea of downward." Up and down are two sides of the same coin; the same is true of advancing and retreating, left and right. This becomes especially important in Tai Chi martial arts applications and strategy. When moving forward, you should always be ready to instantly retreat if necessary. Similarly, when retreating you should remain watchful for the opportunity to advance. If you concentrate exclusively on advancing without keeping some mindfulness of retreating, you can easily be led into a trap, and your mind will be unable to shift quickly enough to escape because your mind is too yang and you have not maintained the seed of yin in your intent.

If you want to lead your opponent upward, it is good strategy to first apply a slight downward force. Your opponent will tend to try to defend against the false downward attack by moving upward; then you can lead his intention, borrow his energy, and combine it with yours in your upward attack, effortlessly uprooting him.

The same principle holds true with left and right. If you want to attack your opponent's right side, create a diversion by applying a slight force on

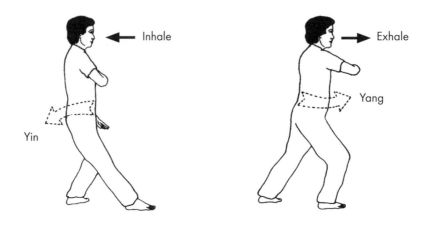

Inhale ← | → Exhale

Yin | Yang

Fig. 7.7 Retracting is yin; advancing is yang

his left side. If his attention then goes to his left, he may leave his right side undefended, making it easy to attack.

SOFT AND HARD

The Tai Chi classics say, "From the greatest softness comes the greatest hardness." Tai Chi Chi Kung is sometimes called a soft-style martial art. This is because most martial arts emphasize strength and speed, whereas Tai Chi emphasizes a balance between soft and hard. Still, it is wrong to characterize Tai Chi merely as a soft style, because the name Tai Chi means yin and yang, both soft and hard. Some Tai Chi students mistakenly cultivate the soft to the exclusion of the hard, ending up with what is disparagingly referred to by the true masters as "tofu Tai Chi."

While most people can easily understand the power of hardness in the martial arts, the power of softness and yielding seems contradictory and confusing. The strength of Tai Chi is compared to refined spring steel. Spring steel is flexible yet strong, yielding yet powerful. To refine iron ore into spring steel, ore must be melted to a soft molten state many times until all the impurities are removed. Similarly, in Tai Chi training the student must first learn to relax and become flexible in every joint until all unnecessary tension and stiffness are refined out of his or her movements. As a result, the student becomes strong yet supple, soft on the outside yet firm on the inside, like steel wrapped in cotton. This is true power, a balance of yin and yang.

The principle of balancing softness and hardness is also applied when dealing with an opponent. We meet the opponent's yang force with yin and attack his yin place with yang. In Tai Chi we never meet the opponent's yang attack head-on. Instead of facing the brunt of an opponent's yang force, we yield to it in a soft, yin way. Because yang always contains yin, we must at the same time scout out where the opponent is soft and yin (weak and unguarded) and apply our yang hard force to that area. We do not waste our yang force trying to confront our opponent's yang directly. Instead, we conserve our yang energy and wait to apply it where it will require the least amount of effort to gain maximum advantage.

Many martial arts styles separate defensive and offensive movements into two separate steps. First they block, then they strike. In Tai Chi Chi Kung, yin and yang, defense and offense, are integrated into every single movement. Defense and offense usually occur simultaneously in Tai Chi. While one hand is yielding, the other hand is striking; when the upper body is yielding, the lower body is attacking.

The Tree Exercise provides a means of emphasizing the subtle energy differences between the yin and yang forces.

Yin/Yang Tendon: Tree Exercise

1. Find a healthy, beautiful tree and begin by directing the Ward Off movement toward the tree, with your right leg and right arm in front.
2. Start with a very slow in-breath. Feel the earth force pulling the sacrum down. The heavenly force produces a corresponding counter-pull upward. Begin to push the right leg into the earth, moving the structure backward without moving the hands.

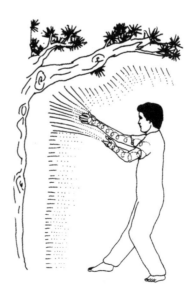

Fig. 7.8 Yin/yang exercise with tree

The feet remain in place. Straighten the right wrist so the palm no longer faces the body but now faces the left side. Position the left hand so the palm faces up.

3. Sink back deeply into the left foot and feel the weight of the entire body being supported by the foot, sole, heel, and hip. As you sink back, bring the left hand under the right hand and pass it along the underside of the right arm until it is just under the right elbow. This position is known as Protecting the Elbow.

   This is the yin portion of the exercise, and so during the sinking the energy is drawn in through the fingertips, through the tendons of the arms, and down through the rest of the tendons of the structure. Focus your attention on drawing the energy from the tree as a rich supply of healthy energy.

   Take care to keep the chest sunk and the arms rounded. Don't allow the right arm to collapse so that it comes closer to the body. In sinking back, often the pelvis gets twisted sideways in the direction of the left leg. A combination of factors causes this to happen: one is rigidity in the muscles and ligaments connecting the hip bone to the spine and legs; another is excessive sinking down so the central line of gravity passes beyond the sole of the left foot. By twisting sideways the center of gravity is somewhat restored but the alignment with the spine is lost. This problem is particularly common among women. Exercises to loosen the hips should be practiced regularly, along with lower abdominal breathing.

4. You begin the yang phase of the exercise when you are fully sunk back. This time the hands do not move at all. Maintaining your position, initiate this phase by slowly exhaling and pressing the left leg into the ground. This creates a force from the opened groin onto the tendons of the legs, which now receive the rebounding earth force. Based on the correctness of your structure, the earth energy travels up the tendons of the legs, past the hips to the C7 vertebra, through the tendons of the right arm and out the fingers toward the tree. Here the tree absorbs the yang energy you are generating.

   Once you have sensitized yourself to the subtle exchanges of yin and yang energies with the tree, you can continue this exercise without losing energy because you are sharing the yin and yang phases of give and take with the tree.

   For consistency, keep the breath inhalations and exhalations corresponding to the yin and yang motions of the exercise. For optimal results, all motions should be as slow and smooth as possible. Corresponding your breath with your movement helps to keep the motions smooth.

YIN/YANG AND INNER SMILE FORM

From the previous discussion you should be able to understand and apply the principles of yin and yang throughout your practice of Tai Chi Chi Kung. Here we provide a step-by-step explanation of the introductory movements to help you get the idea. Apply the principles of yin and yang as you progress from the introductory through the core movements of the Tai Chi Chi Kung form.

INTRODUCTORY MOVEMENTS: WU CHI STANCE

Smile

The inner smile plays a particularly important role in the Wu Chi stance. The phrase *wu chi* translates as Supreme Nothingness or Pure Openness. We begin by smiling to the throat center or parathyroid; this opens up our ability to express. To participate in the interaction of yin and yang, emphasis is placed on the ability to change with grace and smoothness. A person has a general willingness to change when the throat center is open. Smiling in Tai Chi practice expresses a happy connectedness with the universe. Smiling also helps eliminate tension (the kind you get when you have a lump in your throat from anxiety).

Next, smile to the muscles. This helps correct any excess tension caused by unnecessary structural reliance on the muscles and aids in transferring more of the load-bearing effort to the tendons and bones. When the muscles are relaxed away from the bones, the chi can flow.

Finally, smile to the tendons and bones to prepare the body for motion. This is particularly important later on for the proper execution of the Changing the Tendons Form and the Bone-Breathing Form.

Breathing and Drawing Energy

The breath helps direct the phases of the motion. Inhalation is yin, gathering the force, while exhalation is yang, expressing and releasing the force. The breath also acts as a measure of the lesser, greater, and greatest partitioning of the yin and yang cycles. During the course of practicing the entire form, it is essential that the practitioner never run out of breath or be caused to suck in air quickly to continue. Your breath should be as smooth, slow, and even as your motions. It is said that when you control your breath, you control your life.

Paying careful attention to the pulsing in the palms, mid-eyebrow, crown, and soles is useful in coordinating your breath and the chi flow with your

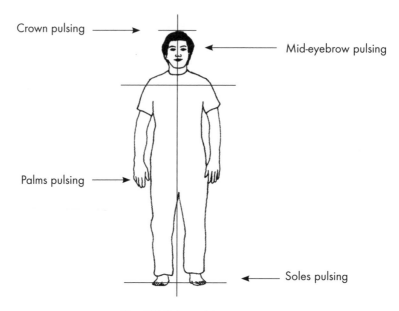

Crown pulsing →

← Mid-eyebrow pulsing

Palms pulsing →

← Soles pulsing

Fig. 7.9 Point pulsing

motions. You should also pay attention to the pulsing in the joints when you are in the Wu Chi stance, especially in the spinal joints.

OPENING TAI CHI

Preparation

The weight transfer begins by sinking down onto the right leg. Lighter weight is yin and heavier weight is yang. Also, left is yin and right is yang, as it is naturally in the body. These right and left roles are reversed during the transitions into the various directions. The back maintains the connection between earth (yin) and heaven (yang).

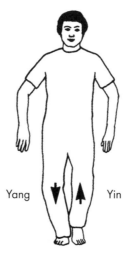

Fig. 7.10 Preparation

Yang   Yin

Step Out

Stepping out leads to an equal distribution of weight between the legs, a balance between yin and yang. This phase emphasizes Wu Chi, the nothingness that exists beyond yin and yang; it is the subtle equipoise from which yin and yang later emerge as Tai Chi.

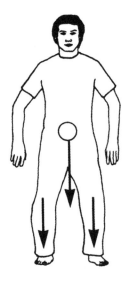

Fig. 7.11 Step Out: balance of yin and yang

Raising the Arms

The fingertips, facing downward, connect with the earth energy and draw in the cool, healing, blue, electric-like current during the yin phase of Raising the Arms. This is followed by the yang phase, where the arms move outward and lightly float up toward heaven. When the wrists reach shoulder height, a transition to yin begins as the arms bend and contract inward in preparation for the Two-Hand Push.

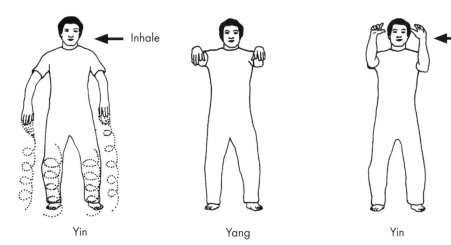

Yin   Yang   Yin

Fig. 7.12 Raising the Arms: yin

Two-Hand Push

The rippling action of the Two-Hand Push is the yang action of guiding the earth energy up through the body and out in the direction of the push. Iron Shirt Chi Kung II particularly emphasizes this skill; the tendons conduct the energy flow in synchrony with the chi pulsing.

Begin the motion by pressing the nine points of the feet into the earth, creating a wave that travels up through the knees, groin, and hips to the sacrum. Relax the psoas and tuck the sacrum at just the right moment to propel the wave up your spine to C7, where you increase the wave by tucking your chin and then direct it out the shoulders, elbows, and wrists to the palms. Completely direct the motion by the tendon power of your whole body; the hands never move independently.

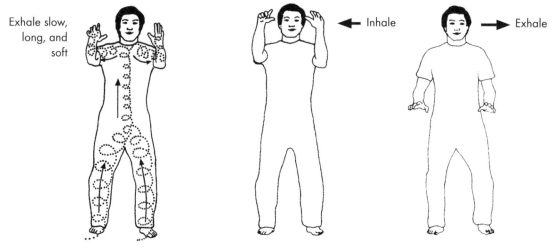

Fig. 7.13 Two-Hand Push exhale: yang

Fig. 7.14 Raise the arms and inhale: yin

Fig. 7.15 Bring hands down and exhale: yang

Lowering the Arms

The yin phase involves gently retracting the tendons and bringing the wrists back in toward the body, still at shoulder level. Then, with arms relaxed and passive, exhale and let the earth force of gravity draw the arms down to the level of the hips.

CONCLUSION

As you can see, there are many aspects to the expression of yin and yang in the Tai Chi Chi Kung form. In the Tao Te Ching it is said that the journey of a thousand miles begins with a single step. The best way to learn the nuances of Tai Chi Chi Kung is to focus on one of these principles at a time. Choose one aspect of yin and yang as described in this chapter and make that the focus of your practice until you have mastered and integrated the principle within all the movements of your Tai Chi Chi Kung form. Then move on to the next principle. In this way, step by step, you will soon master all of the various expressions of yin and yang in Tai Chi movement.

Yin/Yang and
Inner Smile
Form

Rooting and Grounding: Connecting with the Earth

WHAT IS ROOTING?

One dictionary definition of *root* is "the source or origin of an action or quality." This definition echoes the Tai Chi classics: "Each movement is rooted in the feet, developed in the legs, directed by the waist, and expressed through the fingers and hands."

The physical process of rooting involves aligning the skeletal structure with gravity. The resulting connection with the earth allows for a free exchange of force down through the skeletal structure into the earth and back up from the earth through the structure.

Rooting is essential to all aspects of Tai Chi Chi Kung: defending, neutralizing, and attacking. In terms of defense, the ability to redirect any horizontal force vertically into the ground makes a rooted person nearly impossible to push over. The effect is similar to driving a stake into the ground. The more pressure you apply, the more firmly the stake is driven into the ground.

Neutralizing or deflecting can be accomplished from a rooted position without the risk of being knocked off balance. The power for all offense, such as Ward Off, Push, and Press, comes from the flexion and subsequent extension of the legs.

The leg muscles are the strongest muscles in the body. In many Western societies they have become little more than a means for conveying the head and arms from place to place; however, the leg muscles play a significant role in Tai Chi Chi Kung. Ninety percent of the force in Tai Chi Chi Kung comes from the legs. This force cannot be used unless it is supported by a stable base in the feet. If the feet are not properly positioned, the body becomes like a tree with half of its roots damaged. Such a tree would have difficulty drawing enough nutrients up from the soil; it would also be susceptible to being blown over in a windstorm.

WU WEI AND ROOTING

A goal of Tai Chi Chi Kung is to produce maximum force with minimal effort. The Taoists call this principle Wu Wei, effortlessness. Hence, the emphasis in Tai Chi Chi Kung is on relaxing the muscles and shifting the load-bearing effort to the skeletal structure and tendons. Excess tension drains energy; correct Tai Chi Chi Kung practice generates energy and increases chi. This surplus of chi then becomes available for healing or spiritual work.

Higher levels of spiritual work involve drawing in large amounts of heavenly yang energy. People who do not have an effective way of grounding that energy and balancing it with the yin earth energy may resort to using drugs, sex, alcohol, and overeating to get the yin energy they need. Many of the well-known Tai Chi masters of the past fell victim to these vices in a misguided attempt to balance their excess yang. However, these activities have negative health consequences. In the Universal Tao, because of the emphasis on drawing in the pure yin energies of the earth while rooting, the practitioner can do higher-level meditations without abusing drugs, sex, alcohol, or food. In my book *Iron Shirt Chi Kung*, I give point-by-point descriptions of how to connect the whole structure. Readers are referred to that book for further reference on aligning and grounding.

The skeletal structure is designed to distribute the weight of the body evenly over the nine points of the foot. If you were to put ink on the soles of your feet and step on a piece of paper, the nine points would be revealed in the print: the heel point, the outer edge of the foot, the small ball, the large ball, and the five toes. Distributing the body's weight evenly among these points provides a stable foundation for the rest of the structure.

By contrast, uneven weight distribution results in instability, unnecessary tension, and loss of power. One indication of uneven weight distribution is the wear pattern on shoes. Shoes that have been worn for a while develop uneven wear patterns if one part of the foot is habitually stressed more than other parts.

The importance of the connection the feet make with the ground is recognized in sports. Shoes are now designed for specific sports; it seems that every sport has its own shoe design. Each shoe manufacturer attempts to develop a model that will give its wearers a competitive edge. Shoes for sports performed on grass even have cleats to help players root to the ground. In Tai Chi Chi Kung, a similar result is obtained by applying knowledge of anatomy.

Not using all nine points of the foot is like leaning back in a chair so that only two of the chair's legs are touching the ground: the resulting position is unstable. Attention that could be focused on the task of sitting stably on the chair must be diverted to maintaining balance. That task also requires unnecessary muscular effort.

Not standing on all nine points of the feet is like running a galley ship in which only half the oarsmen row. Only half of the available manpower goes into moving the boat, and the oarsmen who do not row are gradually weakened by inactivity. Hence, an already reduced source of power continues to diminish. Tai Chi practitioners who break their root significantly decrease their power by rolling off their base of support so that the heel, the toes, or the outside edge of the foot comes off the floor.

ROOTING EXERCISES

 ## Tai Chi Walking

It is good to be aware of your feet as you walk during the day. The following exercise will help you be more conscious of your feet in walking.

1. Step forward, touching the heel down very lightly before shifting weight onto it.

2. Slowly roll onto the outer edge of the foot, then onto the small ball under the little toe and the large ball under the big toe. Then roll onto the toes: the big toe, second, third, fourth, and little toes. Feel your weight evenly distributed between both balls of the foot and all five toes.

3. Shift your weight back to your rear foot. As you do, be mindful of keeping the nine points of your rear foot flat on the ground. Be sure not to lift your heel.

4. Lift the toes, small ball, large ball, and outer edge of the front foot off the ground, then rotate your front foot out 45 degrees.

5. Roll onto the front foot; shift all your weight to that foot. Balance and step out straight with the free foot, touching your heel down first very lightly.

Fig. 8.1 Tai Chi Walking

Fig. 8.2 Tai Chi Walking: forward

Fig. 8.3 Tai Chi Walking: foot inward

Fig. 8.4 Tai Chi Walking: foot outward

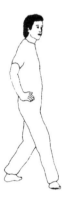

Fig. 8.5 Tai Chi Walking: weight on heel

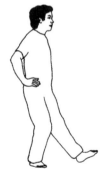

Fig. 8.6 Tai Chi Walking: shifting

6. Repeat steps 2 through 5 up to twenty times. With each step, sense the nine points touching the ground. When you press the nine points to the ground and relax, you activate the earth force. When you are aware of the bones and the nine points and you relax, you will gradually feel the earth force transform from the ground up into the bone structure.

*Rooting and
Grounding:
Connecting with
the Earth*

145

The relaxation phase is very important. Rest and feel the energy. The more you relax, the more easily you will feel the force; the more you tense, the more the muscles clamp into the bone and the harder it is for chi to flow. When you relax, chi flows very easily through the bones, the fascial layers, and the muscles. When you press the bones, the bones produce more chi.

This precise manner of stepping is in contrast to the way most people walk, which is a slightly refined version of the way a toddler walks. To begin a step the torso is inclined forward; the person avoids falling by catching the weight on a foot that is rapidly thrown out in front. With each step the entire structure is jarred. Among the organs, the kidneys are particularly adversely affected by this way of walking. Unless you makes a conscious effort at retraining, walking continues to be a process of falling and catching yourself. Contrast this to the instinctive steps of a cat when it is stalking. This manner of balanced movement is what we seek to emulate in Tai Chi Chi Kung.

Spiraling to Weld the Structure Together

Spiraling links the structure of the legs together in a very powerful way. The bones of the hip are connected to the femur (the thigh bone), which connects at the knee to the two bones in the calf (the tibia and fibula), which then join the foot at the ankle.

1. Begin standing with the feet shoulder-width apart, knees slightly bent. Tuck the sacrum and sink the coccyx until the feet press more firmly into the ground. This movement directs the tan tien chi down through the legs into the feet and into the earth. When the upper body is vertically aligned, all of its weight stacks on the hips.

2. Smile to the groin area. Let it loosen until it feels like an empty bucket.

Fig. 8.7 Spiral down the legs and press the feet firmly against the ground

3. Open the groin, pressing out with the upper thigh. This movement initiates a spiral down the legs: counterclockwise down the left leg and clockwise down the right leg.

4. Amplify the spiral at the knees by gently pressing them down and out.

5. The spiraling continues down through the calfs to the ankles to the feet. The feet spiral out. Force is transferred evenly to all nine parts of the foot: the heel, the outside of the foot, the small ball under the little toe, the large ball under the big toe, and the five toes.

⟳ Knee-Twist Practice

1. Assume the Bow and Arrow stance with the left foot back and the right foot forward.

2. Feel the nine points of both feet touching the ground. You can have your weight equally supported by both feet or have 70 percent of the body's weight on the front leg and 30 percent on the back leg.

3. Now become aware of the knees. Press the feet to the ground and slightly twist the left knee counterclockwise and the right knee clockwise. Relax and feel the chi flow up from the earth through the feet, up to the knees, and up to the hips.

4. Repeat a few times, then change legs and repeat with the right foot back and the left foot forward.

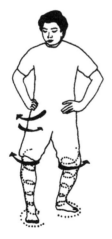 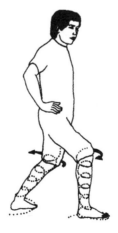

Twist the knee gently outward and feel the force screwing into the ground

Fig. 8.8 Twisting the knees outward

Knee-Twist Practice with a Partner

1. While standing with the knee twisted, have a partner push gently but firmly on the outside of the knee to see how much strength is generated by the spiral in the bones. Have the partner start pushing with one hand and increase to two hands.

2. To emphasize how much the twisting of the knee increases your power, repeat the exercise. This time try not to twist the knee. Press the feet into the ground as hard as you can and have your partner push gently but firmly on the knee. Observe the difference.

SPIRALING MULTIPLIES THE FORCE OF AN ADVANCE

In Tai Chi Chi Kung, spiraling in the legs is emphasized throughout the advancing (shifting forward) movements such as Ward Off, Press, and Push. The feet need to be properly positioned. How far forward the front foot is placed relative to the back foot is determined by how far you can step forward with all the weight still balanced on the rear leg. Attempts to exceed this stepping length result in instability. The two feet should be shoulder-width apart. The rear foot should be at a 45-degree angle to the front foot.

To begin the advance, all the weight should be on the rear leg. The legs are considered one of the three bows of the body. Sinking into the rear leg is analogous to bending the bow. Feel that you are gathering your strength like a horse preparing to jump a stream or fence.

Initiate the movement forward by sinking the groin and connecting the coccyx to the feet. Spiral both legs. When the right foot is forward, the spiral for that leg is in a clockwise direction. When the left foot is forward, the spiral for that leg is in the counterclockwise direction. As you move forward, continue spiraling. Stopping spiraling is like leaking air out of a tire; you lose all the force you have generated.

When your advance is completed, your hips should be square to the front.

ROOTING FORM

In the Rooting Form of Tai Chi you incorporate all the principles and skills you have learned through the rooting exercises. To evaluate your skills, have a partner test your structure in each of the postures as illustrated in this section.

⟳ Opening Movements

Wu Chi Stance

The Wu Chi stance is particularly important for setting the rootedness of the Tai Chi practice. The "nothingness" of the stance can be achieved only with appropriate connection to both heaven and earth, which implies rooting.

The following checks should be made to determine the effectiveness of your Wu Chi stance for rooting.

- The nine points of each foot connect to the ground properly.
- The feet are relaxed and open.
- The muscles are relaxed and the tendons are activated.
- The knees are slightly bent, opening the energy gates to the earth force.
- The groin (the kua, or hip joint) is open.
- The pelvis is square to the north.
- The psoas muscles are relaxed.
- The sacrum and coccyx are aligned to the ground.
- The spine is erect.
- The chin is gently tucked.

In addition, and just as important to a correctly rooted structure, the mind is relaxed. Smile to all the joints that affect rooting: the ankles, knees, and hips. This mental rootedness is required for the energy from the earth to move freely into the stance. Rootedness can be verified each time by sensing a cool and comfortable connection with the blue earth energy.

Once you are in this stance, have a partner place one hand on your shoulder and the other on your hip and push. If your structure and rooting are correct, the force will transfer to the ground.

Fig. 8.9 Correct structure and rooting will transfer energy to the ground

Opening Tai Chi

The Opening Tai Chi movement involves sinking your weight into the earth force. This provides an increased connectedness with the rooting force of gravity. The mind should relate the two as the body sinks by sensing the increased earth pull, as if the weight of the body is actually being brought by the earth toward itself. The transition of weight from one leg to the other allows the practitioner the opportunity to become sensitized to rooting on the left and right legs.

 ## Core Movements: Left-Hand Form

Grasp the Bird's Tail

First Ward Off: Holding the Chi Ball. When you shift weight to the left leg and extend the right leg forward, the distance between the legs plays an important role in the rootedness of your form. You should place your forward leg with a completely opened groin, relaxed to full extension and with the heel touching the ground comfortably. Picture this movement as a drafting compass, with the leg acting as a pencil. Once the groin is opened and the appropriate angle of sweep has been traversed, there is virtually only one correct location to place the heel. If done properly, this ensures that the next yang actions will have a properly rooted stance, which efficiently draws energy from the earth. Without a properly selected position, the stance will be either too wide or too short, leading to poor rooting.

Fig. 8.10 Rooting in First Ward Off

Second Ward Off: Rolling the Chi Ball. In the yang portions of Ward Off the rooting action is most important. The nine points of the feet must have the correct contact on both the front and the back foot. The ankles must be torqued opposite to the knees to provide the necessary activation on the tendons of the ankles. The left knee is lightly twisted counterclockwise and the right knee is lightly twisted clockwise; both are torqued in an outward direction with the force generated by opening the groin. With a tucked sacrum and properly squared hips, the lower structure is then properly rooted and aligned and can act as a conduit of earth energy for the upper body to allow the wave motion to direct the yang action.

Mental sensitization to the spiraling action of the energy up the legs assists in proper rooting to the earth. Also, it is critical that the action begin as an impulse, with the soles of the feet pressing into the ground, followed by an immediate push off the back heel. This creates the impulse that rebounds the earth energy up the tendons of the body. While both feet are used for this purpose, the back foot serves as the primary power source, with the right foot acting as the supportive secondary source.

Rollback. During the Rollback, the feet are stationary and firmly connected to the earth. Feel the energy spiral up through the knees, with the hips and waist carrying the upper body along. This twists the tendons and creates a spiraling of the earth energy. Use the mind to root during this turn so you feel the energy connecting to the earth through the spirals around the legs.

Fig. 8.11 Elbow press in Rollback

Two-Hand Press. The Two-Hand Press uses the same rooting techniques that were described for the Second Ward Off; only the arm action is different.

Two-Hand Push. The Two-Hand Push also uses the same rooting techniques that were described for Second Ward Off. Only the arm action is different, to implement the push.

Single Whip: South

First Twist. Keep the back leg rooted during the torquing action of the pivot. Use your mind to root during the pivot so you feel the energy connecting to the earth through the spirals around the back leg. The back knee leads the way, with the foot locked into the ground as the energy is drawn up the leg in preparation for the strike.

Forming the Beak (Second Twist). When you transfer your weight to the right leg, connect down through the nine points and lock into the earth.

Releasing the Beak (Third Twist). Here you release the torqued force gathered in the right leg. The left foot disconnects when it is raised on the balls of the foot, such that the full storage of power is in the right leg just prior to the strike. Feel the spiral from the foot through the leg. Open the right groin and feel the spiral continue up through the trunk, through the shoulder, and out into the right arm. The right foot should remain locked with the nine points rooted into the earth, so the energy is effectively released with the beak.

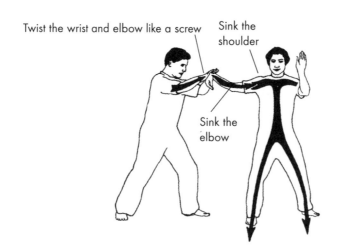

Fig. 8.12 Beak press in Releasing the Beak

Reaching Up to Heaven. Once again, the distance the leg sweeps out is particularly important to the rooting of the yang actions that follow. The leg should be straight, with the groin open and the heel of the foot placed lightly on the ground in a fully extended position. When the foot screws down into

Fig. 8.13 Shoulder press in Reaching Up to Heaven

the ground and the weight shifts between the left and right legs, pay special attention to mentally rooting into the ground as the yang action reaches up to heaven.

Single-Hand Push

Like the previous yang actions, the Single-Hand Push has the same rooting as was described for Second Ward Off. The only difference is the action of the arms to implement the push.

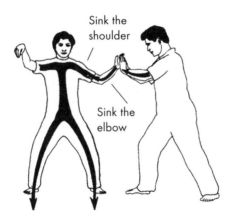

Sink the shoulder

Sink the elbow

Fig. 8.14 Hand press in Single-Hand Push

Transition Movements

Protecting the Chest

The Protecting the Chest action, like the Single-Hand Push, has the same rooting as was described for Second Ward Off. The only difference is the action of the arms to implement the protection of the chest.

Holding the Baby

The nine points of the feet are locked into the earth during this motion to maintain the rootedness that was set up by the Single-Hand Push to the north.

Closing Movements

Cross Hands

It is particularly important when stepping backward that you step in a graceful, balanced, and rooted way, like a cat walking. The sinking, followed by the slow extension of the knees, is performed while keeping in mind your firm connection to the earth.

Hun Yuan Stance

The Hun Yuan stance is completed with rootedness in exactly the same manner as at the start of the form.

Transferring Chi Through the Body

MOVING THE FORCE THROUGH THE SPINE

The goal of connecting to the earth force by rooting is to bring the energy from the feet all the way up to the hands. Although the feet and legs are the structural foundation, having structure in the lower body is not enough in itself. The force that we have developed in the legs through rooting practice can get jammed in the curved parts of the spine. The antidote is to straighten the three curves of the spine: the lumbar curve, the thoracic curve, and the cervical curve. Force will then transfer smoothly through the straight spine.

A straight spine is like a straight stick. Pushing on this stick will drive it into the ground. The harder the push, the deeper the stick will go. On the other hand, pushing hard on a stick with a bend or kink in it will break the stick.

To straighten the spine, we emphasize working from the coccyx and sacrum upward. The coccyx and sacrum form the lowest part of the spine. When the sacrum sticks out, the space between all the vertebrae in the lumbar spine close, compressing the vertebral discs and stopping the transfer of force up the spine. When the sacrum is dropped and aligned with the foot, these lumbar vertebrae are opened. The sacrum is aligned to open the lumbar vertebrae, which begins the process of lengthening the spine.

Pushing outward at the T11 vertebra serves to straighten this curve and further elongate the spine. The T5/T6 vertebrae are linked to the rest of the spine by sinking the chest.

The curve of the cervical spine is straightened by pushing back at C7 and the Jade Pillow. The spinal processes are then opened and loosened. Having been transferred up thus far, the force is then transmitted through the scapulae out through the arms to the hands.

The exercises that follow will help you to find the proper alignment of the spine for your Tai Chi Chi Kung practice. Some of these exercises require working with a partner; others you can practice by yourself.

ALIGNING THE SPINE

The Sacrum

Standing with right leg forward, have your partner press a fist against your sacrum. Move the sacrum forward and back until you feel that the spinal vertebrae are aligned and that the sacrum feels heavy, dropped down toward the back foot. Tilt the sacrum under (in). Then push it back slightly, but keep the lumbar region open. Pushing out too far will close the lumbar region.

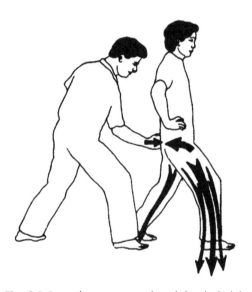

Fig. 9.1 Drop the sacrum and push back slightly

This is the best alignment for the lumbar spine for Tai Chi practice. The lumbar region should feel expanded like a balloon. When the sacrum is properly aligned you will feel the feet pressed more firmly into the ground, as the force of the push is connected to them.

T11: The Thoracic Spine

The eleventh thoracic vertebra (T11) is also called the adrenal center due to its close proximity to the adrenal glands. A good way to find T11 is to find the point midway between the bottom of the sternum and the navel in the front; we call this the solar plexus point. Draw your finger around to the point on the spine opposite the solar plexus; this is T11. If you put your hand on this point and lean forward, you'll notice that it protrudes more than any of the surrounding vertebrae.

Have your partner bring a fist up to T11. Use an inhale to push outward, straightening the curve in the low back and feeling it becoming full and expanded. Push back strongly against your partner's fist, as if you wanted to push your partner backward. Feel the pressure in the feet as the force is transferred to the ground.

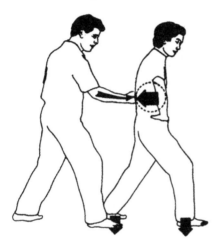

Fig. 9.2 Inhale and push outward at T11, straightening the curve in the low back

Fig. 9.3 Pushing at C7 with the palm

C7: The Cervical Spine

The seventh cervical vertebra (C7) is the lowest vertebra of the cervical spine. This is the big bone at the base of the neck. The Chinese name for C7, Ta Chui, translates as "big vertebra."

Have your partner push on C7 with a palm (not with a fist). The best way to align the spine here is to simulate stopping suddenly in your car: push the feet into the ground, straighten the legs, grab the steering wheel tightly, lock the elbows, and push the chin in and the C7 and Jade Pillow out. Ordinarily we don't exercise the neck like this, but with practice you will automatically have this response; it could save your neck in a traumatic situation.

Jade Pillow: The Base of the Skull

Have your partner put the palm of his or her hand on the Jade Pillow, at the base of your skull. Your partner should be careful not to apply too much pressure to this point; have your partner give only the lightest resistance. Push back, generating Jade Pillow force by pulling in the chin while simultaneously lifting the crown.

Fig. 9.4 Pushing at the base of the skull

Solo Spinal-Alignment Practice

1. If you don't have a partner to help with your spinal-alignment practice, you can use a wall. Stand with the feet parallel and shoulder-width apart, the spine touching the wall. Relax the sacrum.

2. Press the feet to the ground. Twist the knees outward, square the hips, and press the sacrum to the wall. Hold for a while and relax. Feel the chi flow up to the sacrum.

3. Maintaining this position of the sacrum, press T11 against the wall. Hold for a while and relax. Feel the chi flow up to the sacrum and T11.

4. Sink the sternum, push the chin in, round the scapulae, and bring C7 near the wall. Hold for a while and relax. Feel the chi flow up through the sacrum, through T11, and through C7.

5. Finally, generate Jade Pillow force by pulling in the chin while simultaneously lifting the crown. Relax and breathe, feeling the chi flow from the earth through the spine and the crown to the heavens. This is the optimal alignment for your Tai Chi practice.

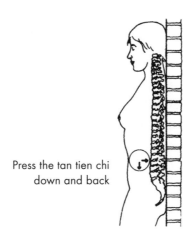

Press the tan tien chi
down and back

Fig. 9.5 Spinal alignment

Fig. 9.6 Spinal alignment on the wall

 ## Spinal Alignment Floor Exercise

1. Lie down on the floor. Feel the spine touching the floor. Draw both knees up and feel the feet touching the ground.
2. Press the feet to the ground and feel the sacrum, the spine, and the head move by the pressing of the feet. Repeat a few times, observing how the feet can move the whole body. Relax and feel the chi flow.
3. Now press the feet to the ground again. Press the sacrum and T11 to the ground. Feel the alignment of the spine.
4. Extend both arms, sink the chest, push the chin in, and feel the C7 point touch the ground. Relax and feel the chi flow.

Press the tan tien chi to the back

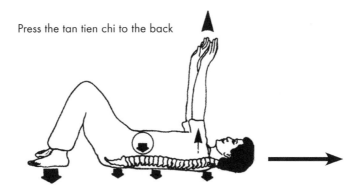

Fig. 9.7 Spinal alignment on the floor

*Transferring Chi
Through the Body*

SINKING THE CHEST

Sinking the chest is an important part of rooting and is especially useful when someone pushes you. He may expect you to be knocked off balance, but if you can root, you can come back with another technique right away.

Sinking the sternum forces breath into the back of the lungs and automatically directs energy down into the abdomen. When the sternum is gently sunk backward, you breathe more into the lower tan tien, draining all body tension downward.

The spinal cord is like the drive train of a car. The hips are the back-wheel drive of the body; the scapulae are the front-wheel drive. When you properly connect these two you have a four-wheel-drive "vehicle"; integrate them and you can efficiently transfer force through the body. This is called locking the structure. When the structure is correctly aligned, you can take a lot of force in and discharge an equivalent amount.

The hips transfer weight to the ground. The earth force comes up through the feet and legs to the hips and through the spine; the scapulae transfer that force out to the hands. Alternatively, force can be transferred from the hands down through the structure to the feet and into the earth.

Sinking the Chest

1. Ask your partner to put his or her hand on your sternum (your breastbone) at the center of your chest. Stick the chest out in an exaggerated fashion.
2. Have your partner gradually push on the sternum but don't let that force move you backward. Instead, exhale to sink the chest and round the scapulae and back. Transfer the force down the front of the body to the

Fig. 9.8 Sinking the chest to align the skeletal structure and direct energy to the tan tien

ground. Feel the nine points of the feet being pressed more firmly into the ground.

3. This is the best position for the chest to aid in aligning the spine and for efficiently transferring force in your Tai Chi practice.

SCAPULA AND ELBOW CONNECTIONS

Scapula Connection

What we call the shoulder is actually made up of three bones: the scapula (the shoulder blade), the clavicle (the collarbone), and the humerus (the upper-arm bone). The shoulder is designed for free range of movement, so the only place the shoulder is actually attached bone to bone to the rib cage is at the point where the clavicle attaches to the top of the sternum (the breastbone). The scapulae themselves float over the rib cage in the back, attached only to the clavicle and humerus. This gives the advantage of flexibility and increases the range of motion of the shoulder. The disadvantage is that because this joint structure is so flexible and free, it can easily become a place where we break or lose structural integrity.

In Tai Chi we need to be able to direct and connect the force we have generated in the legs and hips up the spine and out into the arms. To accomplish this, we round the scapulae. Rounding the scapulae is accomplished by sinking the chest, pulling the chin in, pulling C7 and Jade Pillow back, and separating the two scapulae as far apart as they can go. By doing this the shoulder moves forward and the scapulae press firmly against the rib cage, joining strongly or

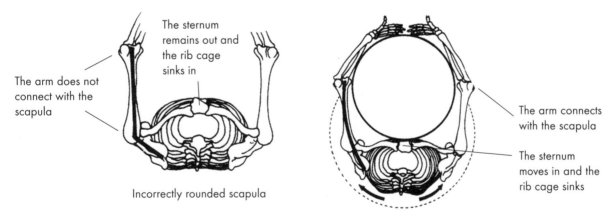

The sternum remains out and the rib cage sinks in

The arm does not connect with the scapula

Incorrectly rounded scapula

The arm connects with the scapula

The sternum moves in and the rib cage sinks

Fig. 9.9 Rounding the scapulae is important for transferring force into the arms. The drawing on the right shows the correct form for the scapulae.

"sticking" to the rib cage and no longer protruding back. From the top view, the upper back appears rounded and the scapulae will feel powerful.

Many animals naturally use scapular power. A tiger walks with scapular power. When it claws, its incredible energy comes from moving the scapulae.

⟳ Scapulae Connection Floor Exercises

Exercise 1

1. Lie on the floor on your back. Raise your knees up. Rest your feet on the floor approximately shoulder-width apart.
2. Raise your arms until they are perpendicular to the floor, pointing toward the ceiling. Keep the arms straight and, for this exercise, lock the elbows. (In the actual Tai Chi form, you would never lock the elbows.)
3. Feel the scapulae touching the floor.
4. Keeping the arms straight, lift the scapulae as far from the floor as possible. Notice how this moves the hands several inches closer to the ceiling.
5. Lower the scapulae to touch the floor, keeping the arms straight and pointed up.
6. Repeat steps 4 and 5 several times. Experiment with doing this movement slowly and then quickly, but never with excess strain.
7. When finished, lower your arms down to the sides. Rest and feel the chi flow.

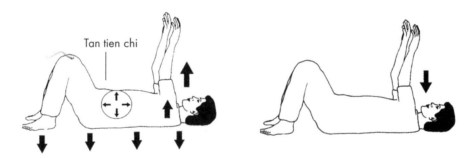

Fig. 9.10 Scapula connection exercise 1

Exercise 2

1. Begin in the same position as in exercise 1. Lying on the floor, bend your knees and rest your feet on the floor approximately shoulder-width apart. Raise your arms until they are perpendicular to the floor, pointing toward

the ceiling. Straighten the arms and lock the elbows. (Remember, locking the elbows is just for the purpose of this exercise.) Feel the scapulae touching the floor.

2. Now tuck your sacrum, feeling the feet make a stronger connection with the ground as you do so.

3. Release the sacrum.

4. Now tuck the sacrum again and feel the connection from the feet up through the legs through the sacrum, like a wave of force. Feel the connection/wave on up to T11 and C7. Pull the chin in.

5. Sink the sternum down toward the floor as you raise the scapulae, as you did in the previous exercise. Feel the connection from the feet up through the hands.

6. Lower the scapulae, relax the sacrum, and relax everything else, but keep the arms up.

7. Repeat steps 2 through 6 several times. Feel the wavelike force each time, from the sacrum to the feet and on up to the arms.

8. Bring the arms back to the sides to finish. Rest and feel the chi flow.

Elbow Connection

Once you are able to connect the shoulder to the spine, if you also have all the aforementioned points in line you can move the energy from the ground up and out into the arms. However, the force will never reach the hands unless you have the elbow connection.

In the Tai Chi classics the old masters instruct us to sink the shoulders and elbows. This means that, for most postures and movements, the elbows should point toward the ground.

To get a feeling for this, have your partner hold your arm up by the wrist. Let the arm relax completely. In this relaxed position the elbow will automatically point toward the ground. You are not using any extra energy to hold the elbow in a strained posture, so you can efficiently direct all the force out into the hand.

Another important structural point is that you want to have the elbows fairly straight in a discharging-energy posture, yet not locked. At a minimum, the forearm and upper arm should always be at an angle greater than 90 degrees. At a maximum the elbow can be at nearly 180 degrees, but the elbow joint should still never be locked stiff.

⊙ Transferring the Force from the Ground

1. Start from a back-weighted stance with the arms held in the Push position. Inhale as you sink back.

2. Exhale and advance until you are nearly to the end of the push.

3. As the knee comes over the foot, straighten the spine from the bottom to the top.

4. Tuck the sacrum; feel the lumbar spine connect with the earth.

5. Push out at T11.

6. Sink the chest. Push out at T5/T6.

7. Round the scapulae. Extend the ligaments at the elbows, wrists, and fingers.

8. Pull in the chin and raise the crown.

9. Feel the energy ripple through and then release.

10. Practice this in a very relaxed way, not forcefully. Practice thirty to forty times a day. Practice until the movement becomes natural.

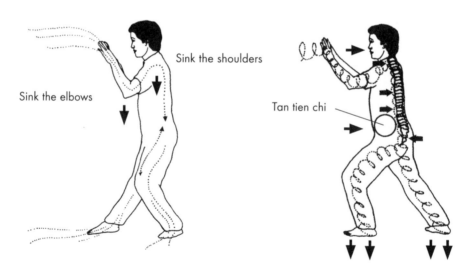

Fig. 9.11 To practice transferring the force up and outward, sink back and then push, pressing the tan tien chi to the ground, opening the groin, pushing back at the spine, rounding the scapulae, and extending the ligaments at elbows, wrists, and fingers.

PUSHING

When you are pushing in Tai Chi, the direction of the chin is determined by the direction you are pushing. When you push to the front, straighten the cervical spine and lift the crown. When you push to the left, turn the chin slightly to the right—just a little bit, not too much. When you push to the right, push the chin a little to the left. When you push the force down, the chin is a little more up.

This movement of the chin when pushing is a very subtle, internal movement.

You can now apply the principles you have learned through these exercises in each of the Tai Chi Chi Kung movements. Make sure the whole body is connected from the beginning of the form to the end. There is not a single movement in which the hands and arms move without the initiation of the rest of the body. You will have mastered this phase when, with every movement, "The power is rooted in the foot, developed in the legs, directed by the hips [and sacrum], clinging to the spine, and expressed through the hands."

Activating the Tendons

WHY THE TENDONS?

Tai Chi practitioners aspire to be like "steel wrapped in cotton." This describes a state in which the muscles are relaxed, as soft as cotton, while the tendons, ligaments, and bones underneath are extremely strong. Mastering the Tendon Activation Form, which involves "changing the tendons," is critical to attaining this quality of steel wrapped in cotton.

Tendons join muscles to bones. Most tendons are composed of dense connective (collagenous) tissue. This silvery white tissue also forms the ligaments (which attach bones to other bones), the deep fasciae (sheets of connective tissue wrapped around muscles to hold them in place), and the membranous capsules surrounding the kidneys, heart, testes, liver, and lymph nodes. Connective tissue is extremely strong yet pliable. The lungs, vocal cords, and

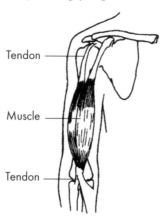

Fig. 10.1 Tendons and muscle

ligaments between successive vertebrae are composed of a more elastic connective tissue.

Medical research has recently discovered the load-bearing function of these connective tissues. The tendons and ligaments can actually bear loads much more efficiently than muscles can. Practical experience in martial arts revealed this fact to the Chinese long ago. Hence, the Chinese emphasize training tendons over building the big bulky muscles that are taken as a sign of physical fitness in the West today.

Maintaining the muscles requires the consumption of large quantities of food, particularly protein. Exercise must be extremely vigorous to increase muscle bulk. This type of exercise would tend to cause one to expend, rather than gain, chi. Overemphasizing the muscles in training eventually results in restricted mobility. Muscle-bound athletes are notoriously inflexible.

Muscles necessarily deteriorate with age, which puts to waste much of the effort spent in building them. By contrast, the tendons, when trained, maintain their strength and flexibility. Furthermore, the rubbery quality of the tendons allows them to store power (jing) when twisted. Maintaining springy, flexible tendons can prevent the stiffness that usually accompanies old age.

Tai Chi Chi Kung uses the body's structure, coordinated by tendon movement, to achieve tremendous power with very little effort. The effectiveness of using the whole body to push an opponent is easily demonstrated. If you were to attempt to push someone using just one finger, you would strain much and accomplish little. Incorporate the rest of your hand by bending your wrist, and you find you can exert more pressure with less effort. Add the force of your entire arm, and you increase your power exponentially.

In the Tendon Activation Form, the tendons and ligaments are used to transmit a wavelike force. The push issues out of the ground and passes through the feet, legs, spine, and arms. The force is multiplied as it passes through the body. With so much force concentrated in so small an area (in this case, one fingertip), real damage can be inflicted.

Training and strengthening the tendons is traditionally called Changing the Tendons. In the Universal Tao system, the complete practice of Changing the Tendons is taught in Iron Shirt Chi Kung II. Changing the tendons does not mean physically replacing them. Instead, the weak tendons are made strong, yet flexible.

The entire physical system, especially the joints, is affected by this training. Over time a weak body is changed into a strong one with an abundant supply of chi. As the joints open they become filled with chi. Chi is led to the marrow and brain to nourish them in a practice called Washing the Marrow,

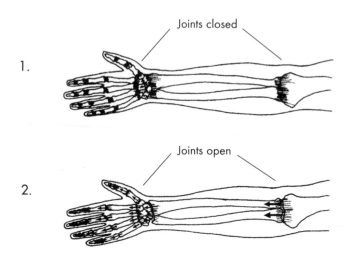

Fig. 10.2 Joint movement in Tai Chi
1. When storing energy prior to discharge, the tendons and ligaments contract, closing the joints. 2. When discharging energy the tendons and ligaments extend, opening the joints. As the joints open they fill with chi, which also serves as a cushion.

which is taught in Bone Marrow Nei Kung, the third level of Iron Shirt Chi Kung.

MIND-EYE-HEART STYLE

The Mind-Eye-Heart style is the most powerful approach to Changing the Tendons. According to an ancient adage, "The I [pronounced *ee*] leads and the chi follows. The chi leads and the body follows." The I is the combination of the mind, senses, heart, and organs together. Throughout the Tai Chi Chi Kung form, the mind-eye-heart is used to lead the chi and move the body.

The heart controls the tendons. When you still the mind and relax completely, you can feel the blood pumping through the arteries as the heart contracts. The Tendon Activation practice involves pairing the movement of the tendons with the heartbeat.

The expanding movement of the tendons can be intensified by using the mind and the eyes. The potential of using mind power to affect bodily processes has recently received attention. Patients who could not be helped by mainstream medical therapies have cured themselves through visualizing diseased parts of their bodies as healthy. Meditations in the Universal Tao system provide experience in moving energy in a seated posture. This experience makes transfer to a moving context, such as Tai Chi, much easier.

The eyes help direct and focus the attention. In addition, the eyes are connected to numerous tendons. By stretching the tendons around the eyes, the tendons throughout the body are activated.

The following exercise provides a way of activating the tendons all over the body. Following this exercise are instructions for activating the tendons in the various movements of Tai Chi Chi Kung.

All-Tendon Action

1. Start in Sink Back position with the hands in Push position.
2. Advance slowly until you are almost fully forward.
3. Listen to your heartbeat. Feel the blood rushing out to the extremities.
4. As you feel the blood pulsing outward, widen your eyes and concentrate the mind. The wave of expansion travels in a manner similar to that described in the Chi Transfer Form detailed in the previous chapter. The movement is from the tan tien down to the ground.

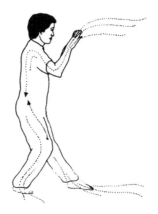

Fig. 10.3 Inhale. Feel the tendons absorb the chi.

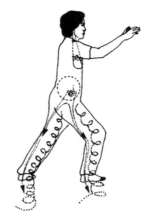

Fig. 10.4 Direct the chi from the tan tien down to the earth. Feel the earth energy extend up the body. Open all the joints and feel the tendons stretch like rubber.

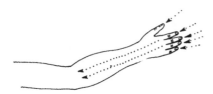

Fig. 10.5 Draw in the chi.

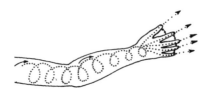

Fig. 10.6 As the tendons twist and stretch, the fingers open and extend. Practicing lengthening the index finger will help open the whole arm joint.

5. From the ground the wave travels up through the feet, legs, spine, arms, and hands. The emphasis is on being aware of the tendons and ligaments and feeling their connection to the mind, eyes, and heart.

6. Once the wave reaches the hands, the tendon stretch causes the fingers to gently separate and straighten. The expansion and contraction of the body is related to chi flow. The chi expands into the hands as the tendons are stretched. During the subsequent contraction, chi is drawn in.

This practice is related to the yin and yang form, which describes the process of exchanging chi, or energy, with the environment. The ability to connect to the earth and draw up earth energy is basic to the Tendon Activation Form. Also, the movement of the spinal cord (learned in the Chi Transfer Form) exercises the flexible tendons in the spine to accomplish the "wave" on which the chi travels.

ACTIVATING THE TENDONS IN TAI CHI CHI KUNG

 Introductory Movements

Wu Chi Stance

The most important part of this stance, beyond the proper alignment of structure to facilitate tendon action, is the coordination of the chi pulse that is flowing through the tendons with the breath and the heartbeat. The pulse can be initially sensed at the palms, mid-eyebrow, crown, perineum, and soles of the feet. However, after an initial sensitization to the pulse timing you should place your attention on the joints of the wrists, elbows, hips, knees, and ankles to feel these activation points open.

Breathing rhythmically, combined with smiling to the body with a men-

Fig. 10.7 Wu Chi stance. Feel the pulse in the heart, palms and soles, mid-eyebrow, crown, and perineum. Feel all the joints opening and expanding.

tal emphasis on opening the joints, relaxes the practitioner and prepares the tendons to be utilized as guides for the chi energy assimilated during the practice.

Opening Tai Chi

The importance of letting the weight of the body be supported by the tendons as opposed to the muscles cannot be overemphasized. The best signal to the practitioner that the tendons are being properly utilized is lack of muscle fatigue. At first the tendons might actually ache from lack of use; however, after a short time flexibility and strength are greatly enhanced by relying on the tendons for all of the Tai Chi actions.

Core Movements

Grasping the Bird's Tail: North

Most of the areas of emphasis for tendon activation in this part of the Tai Chi practice have been brought out in the descriptions of the Yin/Yang and Rooting forms. However, now you should concentrate on the degree of tendon rotation and the efficiency of energy recovery and transfer out of the body from the tendons during the yang release phase.

First Ward Off: Holding the Chi Ball. During the weight transfer, pay careful attention to the tendons in the hip, knee, and ankle of the supporting leg. Let the leg muscles relax entirely as the tendons guide the weight to the ground.

Second Ward Off: Rolling the Chi Ball. During this first outward-directed movement, concentrate on the springing action of the tendons that guide the responding earth energy up the legs and through the body to the spine, scapulae, and arms. Specifically, the tendon points of action are the ankles, knees, hips, shoulders, elbows, and wrists. As your concentration improves, you can incorporate the tendons of the knuckles of the toes and fingers as well as the collarbone.

Rollback. The tendon action here is contained in the knee, which leads the action of the hips, which themselves carry the upper body as one unit. As the knee moves, the feet remain in position; the tendons wrap from the ankle to the knee. This action should be felt and maximized during the practice. Feel the additional twisting action as the knee is moved before the hip, wrapping the tendons around the femur (the thigh bone). Then, with the groin opened, the hip begins to move, creating a twisting action in the tendons that run up

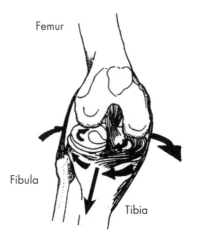

Fig. 10.8 Spiraling of the knee joints

Femur

Fibula

Tibia

the side of the body. At maximum extension, finally the upper body follows until the navel points at 90 degrees (to the west).

Two-Hand Press. The same considerations described for Second Ward Off apply to the Two-Hand Press.

Two-Hand Push. As with the Two-Hand Press, the same considerations that were described for Second Ward Off apply to Two-Hand Push.

Single Whip: South

Single Whip involves the "triple twist." This means that it is also tendon intensive in its application. Here a force is generated by wrapping the tendons around the entire length of the body.

Pivot. Transfer the weight to the tendons of the back leg to support the entire body. As in Rollback, the knee that is turning the body leads as it wraps the tendon around the lower leg from the ankle. At full rotational extension, the tendon of the femur is fully wrapped.

Forming the Beak. The hip moves to create a twisting action on the right side of the body, where the upper body follows to a full turn to the right. Here, too, the weight is transferred to the opposite leg; this requires a smooth transition from one set of tendons to the other so that the motion is slow and graceful. The twisting action of the legs during the creation of the beak is identical, but in the opposite direction. However, the arms and the bent wrist of the beak add an upper-body tendon contraction from the shoulders to the elbow, wrist, and fingers of the beak hand.

Fig. 10.9 In turning, make a smooth transfer of weight from one set of tendons to the other.

Releasing the Beak. In this portion of the practice, the fruits of the newly strengthened tendons and fully coiled body can be tested as an effective weapon. When the action is slow, the attention to the release and extension of the tendons lets you realize the power that the beak-release movement contains.

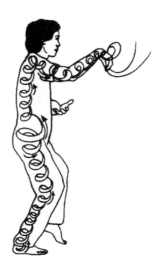

Fig. 10.10 Tendon power releases when turning.

Reaching Up to Heaven. During this action, be sure that the motion of the tendons of both legs and arms are not rushed and that the yang action initiated in Releasing the Beak is carried over into the next motion of the Single-Hand Push via the tendons.

Single-Hand Push. The tendon functions here are identical to those of Second Ward Off.

Transition to a New Direction

Holding the Baby

When you hold a baby—which is done most efficiently with the tendons of the arms as well as the legs—the actions need to be smooth and graceful. This should be the concern during this portion of the practice, letting the tendons be powerful yet gentle.

 Right-Hand Form

The actions of the tendons of the Right-Hand Form are the same as described above except that they occur on the opposite sides of the body. In Tai Chi, all the tendons must be equally exercised to change the tendons so that the weaker tendons become equal to the stronger ones.

Concluding Movements

At the end of a Tai Chi practice, the energy must be collected in the tendons and directed in a circulation that unblocks trapped areas of residue. This energy can then be guided via both the tendons and the Microcosmic Orbit to the navel center for storage during the final Hun Yuan spiraling.

Tan Tien Form

All movement in Tai Chi originates from the lower tan tien. This important region is responsible for control and balance, two key ingredients in proper Tai Chi execution. Additionally, the chi generated through Tai Chi practice is stored in the tan tien; this energy then becomes a reserve that you can add to each time you practice.

While the tan tien is both source and container of chi power, the mind acts like a general that issues orders to the tan tien for directing that power, and the tan tien is like the army camp that dispatches the troops. To be successful with the Tan Tien Form, the mind must be strengthened and focused and the tan tien must be filled with chi pressure.

The mind's ability to focus and to actually move the chi is enhanced by meditation. The Microcosmic Orbit meditation, Iron Shirt Chi Kung, Healing Love practices, and Tai Chi all involve generating, storing, and circulating chi. It is essential at the end of these practices to collect the energy in the lower tan tien. When the energy is stored in the tan tien, it can be accessed later; if it is not stored, the chi dissipates and cannot be used. Storing the chi is accomplished by spiraling at the navel during the final Hun Yuan stance.

We usually refer to the lower abdominal area as the tan tien, but we actually have three tan tiens: the lower tan tien at the abdomen, the middle tan tien (the heart), and the upper tan tien (behind the mid-eyebrow point). Of the three tan tiens, all used in Taoist inner alchemy, the lower tan tien is the most important in Tai Chi Chi Kung. The lower tan tien (henceforth simply referred to as the tan tien) is located in the abdomen approximately three finger-widths below the navel toward the center of the body. The precise location varies from person to person and depends on body type. The tan tien stores our Original Chi, the chi derived from the egg and sperm of our parents and from which our entire organism arises.

Taoist practices emphasize developing and circulating the chi. The tan tien is also called the Ocean of Chi. According to Chinese medical theory, once the ocean is full it overflows into the eight extraordinary meridians. Once these are full, the chi flows into the twelve ordinary meridians, each of which is associated with a particular organ. The tan tien, then, is clearly the foundation of the entire energetic system.

The Tan Tien Form strengthens both the mind and the fasciae to give the practitioner a way of quickly and effectively drawing energy from one area and directing it to another. This skill is particularly useful in other Taoist practices, such as Healing Love, where the energy may be pulling strongly in an undesirable direction (out of the body).

Another way energy can leak out of the body is through urinating. With the Tan Tien practice, if a chi ball is formed and raised away from the bladder area during urination, this indiscriminate loss of energy can be greatly reduced.

As a result of its capacity to deal with large amounts of chi, the tan tien was used as a "laboratory" for inner alchemical work. Translated from the Chinese, the word *tan* means "elixir" (literally "cinnabar," a substance used in outer alchemy as the basis for the elixir of immortality, as it was considered to have the perfect balance of yin and yang). The word *tien* means "field" or "place." The elixir also known as *the pearl* was formed in the tan tien by combining the energies of all the systems of the body, including the organs, glands, and senses. The Fusion of the Five Elements meditation gives precise instructions for forming the pearl.

The following are some preliminary exercises in the Tan Tien Form. We will then move on to working with the Tan Tien Form in Tai Chi Chi Kung.

❧ Tan Tien Breathing

1. Stand in Horse stance, arms curved, palms facing the tan tien.
2. Be aware of the palms and soles. Shoot energy into the navel from the palms as though they were two lasers.
3. Feel the tan tien begin to expand. Allow the hands to expand away from the body as the tan tien expands.
4. Pull the lower abdomen in, condensing the energy in the tan tien. The hands are drawn closer to the body as the navel is drawn in.

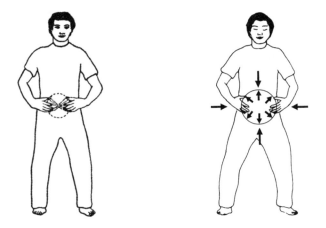

Figs. 11.1 Expanding the chi ball

5. Feel as though you have a chi ball in your belly. Feel the chi ball expand as you inhale. As you exhale, feel the chi ball contract and condense.
6. Continue breathing in/expanding and breathing out/condensing twenty to thirty times, until you feel the chi ball become quite substantial.

Leading Your Movements from the Tan Tien

1. Step forward into Bow and Arrow stance with the right foot, keeping the weight on the back leg.
2. Shift forward by pressing into the ground with the left foot and feeling the ground force come up and expand the chi ball.
3. Shift back to the left foot, feeling that the chi ball is leading the movement by contracting.

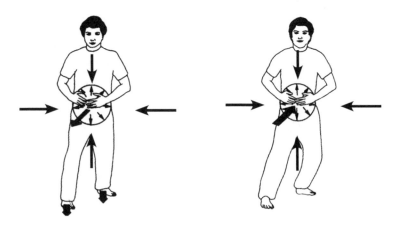

Fig. 11.2 Pushing the chi ball forward   **Fig. 11.3** Turning the chi ball

4. Turn to the left, leading the movement with the turning of the chi ball at the tan tien. You should be able to feel that the chi ball in the tan tien initiates and leads all your movements, whether forward or back, left or right, diagonally upward or diagonally downward.

WORKING WITH THE TAN TIEN IN TAI CHI CHI KUNG

 Introductory Movements

Wu Chi Stance

During this portion of the practice you will create a chi ball in the tan tien, which will then be moved around in the succeeding movements. Smiling is very important to creating the chi ball. Just as the pearl is created in the Fusion meditation, the glands and organs must relax and release their energies, as they do with the Inner Smile, so that the mind can direct these energies to the tan tien. There they can be used as a powerful force for healing and exchanging energy with the environment.

To create a bucketlike storage area for the energy you release as you relax, lower the thoracic diaphragm to create a pressing action on the tan tien. This action pushes the chi ball down as you simultaneously gently pull the sexual organs and anus up. The pressure from above and below compacts and fills the chi ball in the tan tien.

When you are ready to begin practicing the form, divide the chi ball in

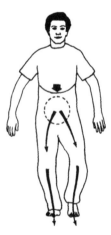

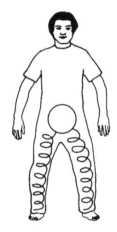

Fig. 11.4 Divide the chi ball and press it down the legs. This will make you feel rooted.

Fig. 11.5 When you relax, the earth energy will rise up the tan tien.

two, sending one part down each leg into the ground to establish better rooting. Once you are rooted, draw in earth energy by bringing the two halves of the ball back up the legs to the tan tien and reunite them to re-form the chi ball.

Opening Tai Chi

After stepping out, reestablish your connection to the ground. Concentrate on the additional power that the chi ball gives to the structure while raising the arms. Move the chi ball forward and expand it to the front while performing the first Two-Hand Push. Feel the energy both pulling up force from the ground through the legs and pushing out force through the arms to the palms. Expand the tan tien area not only in the front but at the sides and low back as well, as if you had a beach ball in your abdomen.

As you draw back and lower the arms, sink down and push the chi ball down toward the coccyx, sacrum, and perineum. This creates an emptiness above the chi ball that can be filled by chi newly drawn through the arms during this yin phase. It also creates a better connection with the earth.

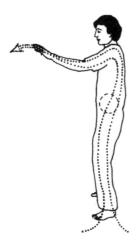

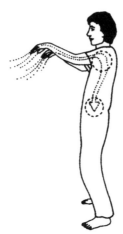

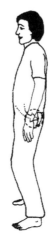

Fig. 11.6 Move the chi ball from the navel to the arms.

Fig. 11.7 When lowering the arms, draw the energy through the arms and bring it to the tan tien.

Fig. 11.8 When the arms are down, push the chi ball to the coccyx.

As you transition the weight during turns, the chi ball is moved to the side of the turn; this acts to massage the left kidney, the spleen, the stomach, and the pancreas, and the descending colon when turning to the left and the liver, gall bladder, and ascending colon when turning to the right. Each transition passes the chi ball over the small intestines and the transverse colon, massaging them as well.

The Tan Tien Form differentiates between the Left-Hand Form and the Right-Hand Form only by the side of the body toward which the chi ball is passed. This becomes self-evident in the course of practice; therefore, only one corner of action is described here.

Grasping the Bird's Tail: North

First Ward Off. During this portion of the form, as the hands rotate and you sink back into a yin phase, move the chi ball back against the spine to massage the kidneys.

Second Ward Off. As the hips turn to the right, pass the chi ball to the right side to press on the right kidney. Then, as you begin the yang, forward Ward Off motion, move the chi ball to the front right side, pressing on the right side of the bladder and sexual center. This enables the outward motion of energy to proceed from the tan tien up to the arms and out through the palms.

Rollback. During the Sink Back movement, lower the chi ball toward the coccyx, sacrum, and perineum; this creates a void that will be filled by energy newly drawn in through the fingers and palms of the hands down the arms to the navel. Reinforce the turn to the left side with the motion of the chi ball

Fig. 11.9 Rollback and Press

toward the back and left kidney; this also draws in additional energy from the raised right hand.

Press. As you return the chi ball to the front of the body for the Press, press the chi ball toward the bladder and sexual center, creating a connection between the ground and the direction of force.

Two-Hand Push. The Two-Hand Push has the same chi ball motion as in Press. Assist this forward and backward motion of the chi ball with the sacrum-tilting action.

Single Whip: South

First Twist. Once again, pass the chi ball back in the direction of the pivot; this creates a massaging action on the central internal organs of the body. It reaches the left kidney with a gentle squeezing action as you reach maximum extension.

Fig. 11.10 Single Whip

Second Twist: Making the Beak. Pass the chi ball back to the right kidney as you form the beak. Again, the chi ball approaches the right kidney with a gentle squeezing action as you reach maximum extension.

Third Twist: Releasing the Beak. As you release the beak, pass the chi ball back to the front of the body and begin the yang action of pressing down to the bladder and sexual center to connect the earth energy to the new outward motion of the force.

Tan Tien Form

Reaching Up to Heaven. Bring the chi ball from the right side of the sexual center and bladder to the center, creating the same connection with the ground, now equally distributed over both legs.

Single-Hand Push. Bring the chi ball to the left side of the sexual center and bladder. This completes the yang action by providing the additional earth force directed out the arm to the palm of the left hand.

Transition to a New Direction

Each of the corners is performed with the Tan Tien Form in exactly the same motions as described above for the north direction. For brevity, the descriptions are not repeated.

Holding the Baby

Pass the chi ball from the front of the body in the area of the sexual center and bladder to the back of the spine in the sacrum and coccyx region and then to the front of the body again. This action both reinforces and is reinforced by the sacral-tilting action. It is also a powerful means of drawing additional energy into the void created by pressing the chi ball low into the body; use the upward-turned palms to draw in this additional energy.

Right-Hand Form

As mentioned earlier, there is no difference between the Left-Hand Form and the Right-Hand Form except that the chi ball is on the opposite side.

Concluding Movements

Cross Hands and Closing Tai Chi

During the action of crossing the hands and returning to the Wu Chi stance, recenter the chi ball into the exact middle of the body from whence it came, to the center of balance, the center of gravity, and the center of attention. This brings the practice to completion.

Hun Yuan Stance

In the Tan Tien Form, the Hun Yuan stance is very important. Stand relaxed with the feet together, left palm over the right palm and both over the navel. Direct the total attention to the navel and spiral the energy into the tan tien.

Fig. 11.11 Use the mind and spiral in the tan tien to collect energy.

The importance of gathering and storing the energy cannot be overemphasized. With all the effort and enjoyment of doing the practice, it would be a shame to let all the results leak out by not taking the last step of locking up the energy in the tan tien.

Avoid eating or going to the bathroom for forty-five minutes following Tai Chi practice. All the energy is concentrated in the navel area, and it would be greatly decreased by the digestion and excretion processes, both of which use up a great deal of energy.

12

Healing Form: Connecting the Organs with the Five Directions

DRAW THE CHI OF THE FIVE DIRECTIONS

An important element in learning the Tai Chi Form is sensitivity toward the directional energies. The Inner Smile can help the student in knowing what the feeling of healthy energy is like, in order to draw the complementary energies from the various directions.

The following is a list of the directions and the corresponding major, minor, and sensory organs.

1. North: water element; the energy of the kidneys, bladder, and ears
2. South: fire element; the energy of the heart, small intestine, and tongue
3. East: wood element; the energy of the liver, gall bladder, and eyes
4. West: metal element; the energy of the lungs, large intestines, and the nose
5. Middle: the earth element; the energy of the spleen, stomach, pancreas, and mouth

The way we move in our environment determines our exposure to each of the directions: north, south, east, and west (the Chinese have a fifth direction, the center). Our houses are fixed in terms of compass orientation. We usually sit in the same chair facing the same direction at the table during meals; we favor a particular chair in which we spend most of the evening hours; we sleep with our body aligned in a particular direction, be it north–south or east–west. When we get out of bed in the morning, we always head in the same direction to go to the bathroom; the door through which we exit the house always opens to the same direction; the path leading to the car is invariable. We typically take the quickest route to work. At work, our office is on one side of the building and the desk faces a particular direction. We drive home along the same route to return to a house that has not shifted its orientation while we were gone.

Constrained by our activities within a fixed environment, most of us are overexposed to certain directions and underexposed to others. As the pattern of the typical day is repeated over the course of weeks, months, and years, this overexposure to certain directions and underexposure to others is compounded.

Each direction is associated with a distinct type of energy. Balance and harmony are achieved through maintaining equal proportions of each of these energies. To achieve this goal, the movements in Tai Chi Chi Kung are practiced facing all the directions. In the Healing Form the energy from the four directions and the center are drawn into their associated organs. If you can get in touch with the energy of the five directions every day, you can maintain and strengthen the functioning of your organs. If you do get sick, by connecting with these energies you can heal faster.

The organs also have color, animal, and planet associations. The colors and animals are symbolic of the energy of the directions. Their efficacy in evoking the energies has been made available to us as tools passed down by innumerable Taoist meditators. Using these same color and animal associations helps connect with the associated energies with which the adepts worked.

The same cosmic particles that formed the planets also form the organs. In this sense the planets are considered parents of the organs. The organs' energies can be nurtured by the energy of their "parent" planets.

You can also see the division of the levels of the Healing Form in terms of earth level, human or cosmic level, and heaven level. At the earth-level practice you use the directional forces, animals, and colors to tune in to their associated energies. These energies are drawn into the body through the palms, soles, and perineum.

At the human- or cosmic-level practice, you use the Six Healing Sounds and the chi ball to tune in to the associated energies. These energies are drawn into the body from in front through the mid-eyebrow.

At the heaven level you use the planets and their colors to tune in to the

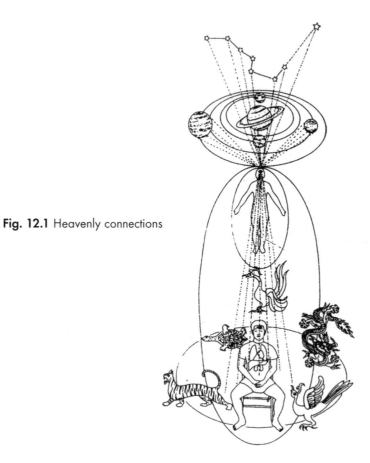

Fig. 12.1 Heavenly connections

associated energies. These energies are drawn into the body through the crown.

For your easy reference, here is a table of the directional associations.

CHI OF THE FIVE DIRECTIONS

Direction	north	east	south	west	center
Element	water	wood	fire	metal	earth
Energy	gathering	expanding	releasing	contracting	balanced
Yin organ	kidneys	liver	heart	lung	spleen and pancreas
Yang organ	bladder	gall bladder	small intestine	large intestine	stomach
Color	blue	green	red	white	golden yellow
Animal	blue tortoise	green dragon	red pheasant	white tiger	golden phoenix
Planet	Mercury	Jupiter	Mars	Venus	Saturn

You must master all the previous levels of Tai Chi Chi Kung before advancing to the Healing Form. When you have reached this level, rooting, spiraling, yin and yang, working through the tendons, aligning the structure, and the other Tai Chi principles will have already become so integrated into your form that you will not have to think about them; they will just happen by themselves, so you are free to relax and absorb the healing energy.

It is also important that you have experience with the advanced level of the Fusion of the Five Elements meditation. This meditation acquaints the practitioner with the various directional energies and their associated colors, planets, and animals.

When first practicing the Healing Form, simply concentrate on the organ associated with each direction. Look up the organs in an anatomy book; know what they look like and what their functions are. Then, during your practice of the form, you can easily visualize each organ. Practicing the Inner Smile and Six Healing Sounds will also give you familiarity with the location of the organs and their energies.

In subsequent repetitions of the form, concentrate on only one association per organ: first color, then animal, then planet. Breathe the color in. Picture the animal coming to you. Picture the planet and feel its energy being absorbed into your cells. After gaining familiarity with the associations in this way, you may combine all the associations into one form.

It is also particularly helpful during practice of the Healing Form to incorporate the Six Healing Sounds. This helps to both tune the mind into the particular energy and stimulate the organ to a healing vibration that will release the negative trapped energies and nurture the virtue energies of the respective organs. For instruction in the Six Healing Sounds practice see my book *Transform Stress into Vitality*.

HEALING FORM PRACTICE

Without repeating the specifics of the Tai Chi Chi Kung form itself, here is a summary of the combined energies of the earth, cosmic, and heaven levels of the Healing Form. You can divide your practice to work up to the combined Healing Form, or you can work with whatever is most apparent at first while developing the more subtle energies next. The most important thing to remember about this form is that it is to be used for total mind and body health. Therefore, proper mental attitude and virtuous emotional control are essential.

When facing a particular direction during practice of the Tai Chi Chi Kung form, absorb energy into the associated organs. Move the tan tien and chi ball to massage those organs. By completing one full course of the Tai Chi Chi Kung form, you will thus activate all of the organs.

Taking time in the Wu Chi stance to smile to your heart fosters a total-body feeling of love, joy, and happiness that sets the tone for your healing practice.

North

You begin the Tai Chi Healing Form facing north. In the north dimension the kidneys and bladder connect with the water element, the earth force, and the blue tortoise. Energetically, the north direction connects with the North Star, the planet Mercury, and the energy phase of gathering and conserving.

Smile and be aware of your kidneys and bladder. Feel the watery quality of gathering and conserving being drawn into you. The bones and teeth are also connected with the north (as they are ruled by the kidneys), so when you collect energy, bring it into the bones and teeth as well. Draw the blue color and the tortoise to you from the earth force on the northern horizontal plane.

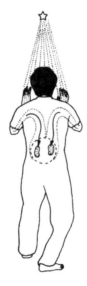

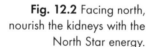
Fig. 12.2 Facing north, nourish the kidneys with the North Star energy.

When you sink back, push the chi ball back into both kidneys. Press into the kidneys using your mind and a slight contraction of the abdomen. When you roll back to the left, press the chi ball into the left kidney, squeezing it. When you roll back to the right, press into the right kidney. When you relax, the kidneys expand, thus drawing more life force into the organ.

The energy of Mercury comes from above. Mercury supplies the kidneys with power. Add the energy of the planet Mercury to the bladder and kidneys. Picture the blue color of Mercury; feel its healing power strengthening your kidneys, your bladder, and your bones.

West

The west side connects with the lungs and large intestine, our major organs of elimination. The energy of the west is associated with the metal element, a very condensed form of energy. When we take this energy into the lungs we receive courage. The associated color is white. When you visualize the lungs and large intestine as you practice the form, you receive more healing.

Smile to the lungs and feel a white force from the west coming to you. Summon a white tiger to give you more energy. Feel the chi ball moving. When you sink the chest and empty the lungs, you can breathe into the lungs and lower abdomen.

When you have a good connection with the west, connect with the heaven force, the planet Venus. Picture the planet and be aware of the white force coming down to you. This requires mind power. Emphasize sinking the chest and emptying the lungs when you push out.

Fig. 12.3 Facing west, draw the energy of the white tiger in the west into the lungs.

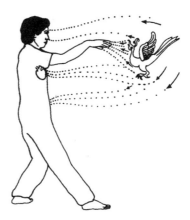

Fig. 12.4 Facing south, draw the fire energy of the red pheasant into your heart.

South

The south connects with the force of fire. The energy is expanding and radiant and helps the heart and the circulation of the blood.

Smile to the heart. Feel the expanding, radiating energy of love. When you feel joyful and happy, expansive and radiant, you will feel wonderful all over. Smile to the heart and the small intestines. The red color is very important for both the heart and the small intestines. Fire is needed to digest food. The heart also needs fire to move the blood.

When you practice the Healing Form facing south, feel the heart radiating a red color. Sink the sternum and be aware of the heart. Call the power of the red pheasant, the animal of the south, to strengthen and protect you. Expand your consciousness outward to the planet Mars. Absorb its red color from above down into your heart.

East

The east is connected with the liver and gall bladder. The color is green. The energy is expansive and growing, like a tree. The tendons are also connected with the east.

Fig. 12.5 Facing east, draw the green energy of the wood element into the liver.

When you roll back, press and massage the liver with the chi ball. Learn to use the tan tien, where the Original Force is stored. When you sink, you come back to the center and press against the spleen. Emphasize sinking back, pressing into the liver and gall bladder.

Call the green dragon, the animal of the east. Be aware of the planet Jupiter. This planet has tremendous energy that can benefit the liver and gall bladder.

Center

The center is associated with the spleen, pancreas, stomach, and earth force. The balanced and harmonizing energy of the center can best be absorbed from the Sink Back, Wu Chi, and Hun Yuan closing positions. No matter which direction you are facing, when you sink back, connect with and absorb the golden yellow energy of the center. Draw the golden phoenix to you, over your head.

Connect with the yellow healing light of the planet Saturn. When you sink down, press the spleen and pancreas with the chi ball.

13

Skin- and Bone-Breathing Form

Because the skeletal framework is the foundation and core of our physical structure, to master Tai Chi Chi Kung the student must learn to activate, energize, and transform the bones and marrow.

For centuries Chinese martial artists have integrated various Chi Kung practices into their training to exercise and develop the bones. In the Universal Tao we introduce these practices within the context of Iron Shirt Chi Kung and Bone Marrow Nei Kung (Iron Shirt Chi Kung III). Within Iron Shirt, the main practices that focus on activating the bones are Bone Breathing, Skin Breathing, and Marrow Washing.

In each of these practices we draw energy into the bones. This removes fat from the bone marrow and creates space for the marrow to grow, enhancing our ability to produce healthy blood cells. The blood cells, in turn, nourish the body and help it to resist disease. The marrow of round bones, such as those of the arms, legs, and spine, produces red blood cells. Red blood cells carry oxygen and nutrients to all the cells in the body. The marrow of flat bones, such as the skull, ribs, and hips, produces white blood cells, the soldiers of the immune system. Healthy blood is thus essential for a healthy body.

These practices also strengthen the bone matrix. The strength of the bone matrix is, in essence, the structural strength of the bones. Bone matrix is the main storehouse of calcium in the body. The bone matrix also stores chi in an unusual way: bone is one of the few substances on earth (along with quartz crystal) that has piezoelectric properties. This means that the electrical charge of the bones increases in proportion to the pressure exerted on the bones.

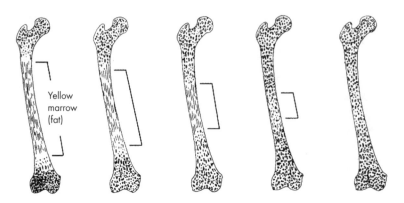

Fig. 13.1 Prolonged Bone Breathing practice helps to clear fat from the bones, nurturing the regrowth of marrow.

Tai Chi Chi Kung is one of the best exercises in the world for pressurizing the bones, because we emphasize shifting the load-bearing job from the muscles to the bones in each and every movement. In addition, we align our entire skeletal structure so that the mechanical force generated in each movement passes through all of the bones. The pressure that is generated enlivens and activates the energy stored in the bone.

The cells making up the bone matrix are some of the liveliest cells in the body. The bone-tissue cells align to each other according to the type of force to which they are subjected. In Tai Chi Chi Kung, the bones are subjected to simultaneous vertical and horizontal forces, which together manifest as a spiral. The result is that the bone cells form into a densely woven spiral lattice pattern, creating incredibly tough bones.

Taoists believe that the cosmic particles we absorb through Skin Breathing and Bone Breathing build up our bodies, cells, and organs. As we draw these particles in, we immediately increase our energy. In Tai Chi Chi Kung we are concerned with the more basic bone-training techniques. My books *Iron Shirt Chi Kung* and *Bone Marrow Nei Kung* give in-depth information on both the bone-breathing process and additional techniques for reinforcing the chi in the bone marrow.

Although Bone Breathing, Skin Breathing, and Marrow Washing all exercise the bone marrow, they do so in different ways. Actually, all of these exercises are often subsumed under the name of Bone Breathing; in the context of this chapter, we refer to them as separate practices.

In Bone Breathing we use the power of the mind to establish a flow of external chi through the fingertips, the toes, and the other protruding bones of the body, spreading it throughout the skeletal structure.

In Skin Breathing the millions of pores and hair follicles in the skin draw in

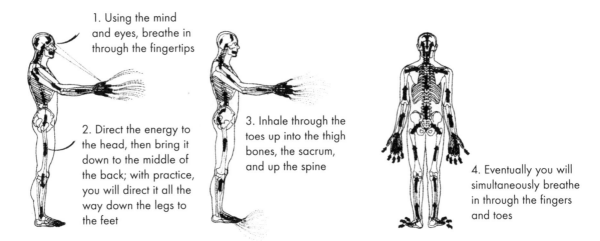

1. Using the mind and eyes, breathe in through the fingertips

2. Direct the energy to the head, then bring it down to the middle of the back; with practice, you will direct it all the way down the legs to the feet

3. Inhale through the toes up into the thigh bones, the sacrum, and up the spine

4. Eventually you will simultaneously breathe in through the fingers and toes

Fig. 13.2 Bone-Breathing practice

energy from the atmosphere. Hair follicles and pores are the most sensitive parts of the body in terms of attracting ions, electrons, and protons from the air. The movement of electrical charge within the body underlies all metabolic processes. On the in-breath, we draw the chi in through the pores and follicles down to the surface of the bone; on the out-breath, we condense the chi into the bones by contracting the muscles close to the bone. We also refer to this process as bone compression.

Skin Breathing and Bone Breathing are efficient supplements to breathing through the nose. The surface area of the skin is far greater than that of the nose alone and therefore has greater energy-drawing potential.

Marrow Washing is a more passive process. With Marrow Washing we draw in external chi, as we do in the previous practices, but unlike in Bone Breathing and Skin Breathing, the absorption of chi is not coordinated with our breathing. In Marrow Washing we open ourselves to receive the downward flow of chi from heaven through the crown and palms, the upward flow

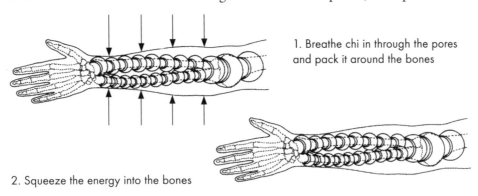

1. Breathe chi in through the pores and pack it around the bones

2. Squeeze the energy into the bones

Skin- and Bone-Breathing Forms

Fig. 13.3 Bone-Breathing practice

of chi from earth through our palms, soles, and perineum, and the horizontal flow of atmospheric or cosmic chi through our mid-eyebrow point. Eventually we absorb chi through all of the skin into the bones, and the practices of Skin Breathing and Marrow Washing blend together. The energy in Marrow Washing is very gentle, like a fine mist of light that steam-cleans and energizes our bone marrow with yin, yang, and neutral energies.

The following are some basic exercises for practicing Bone Breathing, Skin Breathing, and Marrow Washing.

BASIC EXERCISES

 ### Marrow Washing, Bone Breathing, and Skin Breathing

1. Take a very simple stance, such as the Heavenly Stance, with the feet parallel, knee-to-toe-length apart. The arms are raised over the head, elbows bent, palms facing up.

2. Use your mind to draw in the heavenly force. It may appear in your mind's eye as a violet light mist emanating from the North Star. Draw the energy in through your crown and palms and into the bones. Feel the violet mist wash through your bone marrow from top to bottom.

3. Lower the hands so that they are at waist level, palms facing down. This is the Earthly stance.

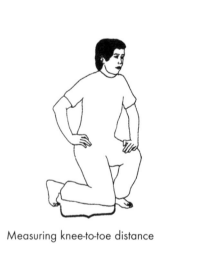

Measuring knee-to-toe distance

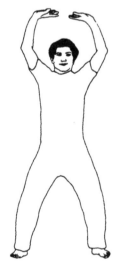

Fig. 13.4 Heavenly Stance

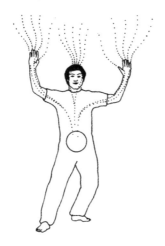

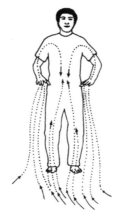

Fig. 13.5 Absorbing heavenly force   **Fig. 13.6** Absorbing earth force

4. Draw up the energy from the earth, the negative charge of Mother Earth, through the soles of your feet, your perineum, and your palms. The earth energy may appear to your mind's eye as a yellow mist. Feel it wash through your bones as if it were steam-cleaning them.

5. When you feel the heavenly and earth forces and have brought them to the navel, focus the awareness on the skin. You can use your hands to lightly rub your skin. Feel the sensations on the skin surface.

6. Inhale, drawing the chi from the atmosphere—ions, protons, electrons, and particles of light—into the skin and down to the outer surface of your bones. Feel your hair follicles acting like lightning rods or antennae, attracting and drawing the energy in.

7. Exhale, lightly contracting the muscles closest to the bone, and squeeze the chi into the bone. Feel it condense into the bones, charging them up. Your bones will feel full, expanded and distended, electric.

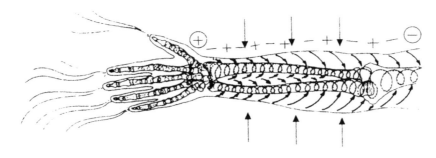

Fig. 13.7 By inhaling though the fingertips and skin, packing, spiraling, and squeezing energy into the bones, an electrical impulse is created.

Skin- and Bone-Breathing Forms

8. Inhale again. Be aware of the kidneys and the sexual center; these centers help absorb particles into the bone to regrow the marrow. Exhale a little bit. Rest, relax your breathing, and feel the skin breathing by itself for six to nine breaths.

⬤ Heaven and Earth Marrow Washing

1. Lower the arms and keep them rounded, palms up, as if you are scooping the energy up from the earth.
2. Inhale and feel the earth energy come up to the soles and the perineum. Slightly contract the anus and inhale energy up to the sacrum. Gradually raise your arms as you inhale up to T11, pushing out the spine slightly. Continue in the same way to T5, C7, the base of the skull, and the crown.
3. Be aware of the Big Dipper and the North Star above you. Inhale. You may feel something very heavy in the crown. Use the heavenly energy to wash the bone marrow. Exhale down. Rest and just feel the positive heavenly charge wash down through the brain, skull, cervical vertebrae, clavicles, and sternum.
4. Draw the energy down through the rib cage and activate the marrow that produces the white blood cells. Draw the energy down the thoracic and lumbar vertebrae to the hips and leg bones. Feel the violet light washing

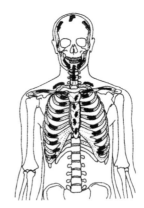

Fig. 13.8 Heaven and Earth Marrow Washing

Fig. 13.9 The heavenly charge washes down the skull and sternum into the ribs.

right through the bones. Just rest and breathe softly, letting the process happen by itself.

5. Rest and continue breathing gently. Be aware of your soles and palms and feel the yellow light rising from the earth; let it wash the bone marrow from the legs up to the sacrum, to the spine (lumbar, thoracic, cervical), to the brain, and up. (The hands have gradually been raised above the head.)

6. Do this exercise ten to twenty times.

Solar Marrow Washing

1. Sunlight, particularly morning sunlight (visualized as violet and yellow), activates bone marrow energy. You can train by looking at the sun at dawn, before its light is too bright. Begin by looking at the sun and blinking your eyes rapidly. Then close your eyes. When you close your eyes you can see violet and yellow. Single out those colors and absorb the energy into the skin and bones.

2. Inhale into the bones and exhale. Relax. Do this for a few minutes, until you feel you have learned the process. Once you have learned the process, the energy absorption can take place automatically.

3. Yellow light from the sun comes down into the bone marrow, washing it, increasing it, strengthening it. Sometimes when you look at the sun you see the red light also. The bones need this too. Visualize that light. On the in-breaths absorb the light in through the mid-eyebrow, the mouth, and the skin. Condense and draw it in to wash the marrow by lightly contracting the muscles near the bone on the out-breath.

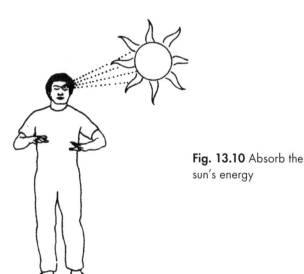

Fig. 13.10 Absorb the sun's energy

Skin- and Bone-
Breathing Forms

🌀 Bone Marrow Inner Smile

1. After performing the Heaven and Earth Marrow Washing, stand for a while and smile to the entire skeletal structure. Take time to smile to each bone one by one.
2. Smile to the skull.
3. Smile to each cervical vertebra. Feel the chi penetrate into each cervical vertebra, filling and expanding the intravertebral space.
4. Smile to the collarbone, scapulae, the humerus, radius, and ulna bones, and the bones of the wrists and hands. Smile especially to the joints in between the bones; feel the chi filling the joint spaces.
5. Smile down to the thoracic vertebrae, the lumbar vertebrae, and the pelvis. Feel the chi filling and expanding the joint spaces.
6. Smile down to the groin (the kua) and feel the chi fill the hip joints. Smile to your femurs, the long bones of the thighs, one of the major bones responsible for producing red blood cells.
7. Smile down to the knee joints and feel the joints fill with chi; smile to your tibia and fibula bones and the bones and joints of the ankles and feet.
8. Rest a moment and feel the entire skeletal structure.

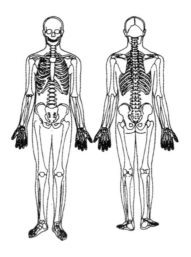

Fig. 13.11 Skeletal structure

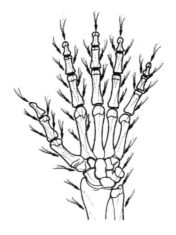

Fig. 13.12 Bones are extremely porous and are always "breathing."

Skin- and Bone-Breathing Forms

INCORPORATING SKIN BREATHING AND
BONE BREATHING INTO TAI CHI CHI KUNG

Introductory Movements

In this early part of the form it is important to take the time to feel all the bones in the body. It is very helpful to look at an anatomy book to familiarize yourself with the look of the following skeletal bones: skull, spine, upper and lower arms and legs, hands, feet, and hips. This allows more accurate visualization during Bone-Breathing practice.

After having become intimately aware of the entire skeleton, move the attention to the heart and kidneys. This activates the spirit and essence energy, respectively. Relax. Feel that you can absorb the energy into yourself.

Inhale energy into the palms, the fingers, and particularly the pores of the skin. It is helpful to view the Bone-Breathing drawings from earlier in this chapter to follow what you can now sense in your body.

Core Movements

In the core movements of the Tai Chi Chi Kung form, which consists of Grasping the Bird's Tail and the Single Whip in the various directions, the mind-eye-heart power (as learned in the Tendon Activation Form) is very important. During the yin phase of each movement, you can draw energy into the skin as you inhale and absorb the energy down to the surface of the bones. The more you relax, the more you draw energy in. During the yang phase you exhale and condense the chi into the bones.

Use the bone structure and breath to reinforce the energy flow. Feel the skeletal structure constantly drawing and then compressing the energy into the marrow; picture the bones and smile to the bones during the entire form.

Sinking back is the yin phase of the movement; begin Bone Breathing by breathing in chi through the tips of your fingers, your palms, and your mid-eyebrow. As you become more accomplished you can also draw in through more areas and centers such as the crown, the tips of the toes, the legs, and the skin.

Shifting forward is the yang phase of the movement; exhale and contract the muscles into the bones, squeezing and condensing the chi into the bones. Feel the energy penetrate deeply into the bones. Picturing the bones as porous, like a sponge, helps this process greatly.

Once you have begun and activated the Bone-Breathing process you can use less effort. Just relax and feel yourself absorbing chi through your fingertips, energy centers, and skin during the in-breath and feel the chi condensing into

Skin- and Bone-Breathing Forms

199

Fig. 13.13 During the yin phase of sinking back, begin Bone Breathing by breathing in chi through your fingertips.

Fig. 13.14 Draw in the chi through both the fingertips and the toes.

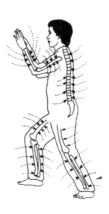

Fig. 13.15 As you shift forward during the yang phase, the bones of your whole body feel porous, like a sponge. Feel all the bones breathing and use your mind to compress the chi into the bones.

Fig. 13.16 Opening the joints during Bone Breathing is a powerful aid to absorbing chi into the bones.

the bones during the out-breath. Continue to be aware of this process throughout your practice of the entire Tai Chi form. Eventually you will use mostly the mind and very little contraction of the muscles to absorb chi into the bones.

You have to go very slowly at this advanced level of practice for the practice to be effective. Draw the energy into the points as shown in the illustrations, slowly and smoothly, as if you are pulling silk from a cocoon; if you pull too strongly, you will break the strand, and if your pull is too weak, it will not give.

The kidneys rule the sexual organs and the bones. The more you can smile into the kidneys and sexual organs, and the slower you go, the more effectively you can draw the energy in.

The yellow, violet, and red colors help rejuvenate the bone marrow. The more you relax with good structure, the more you can feel the chi being absorbed. Feel the skin while drawing energy in and the bones while breathing out. Absorb the energy into the skin, into every pore and hair follicle; you can picture the skin as one big lung. Transfer the force through the spinal cord as described in previous chapters.

Be constantly aware of yin (inhale) and yang (exhale). Actually feel that you are swimming in an ocean of chi, as though you have to push through the chi to create the Bone-Breathing action. When absorbing the chi, you may feel that the chi is very thick. Stay aware of your structure, of the tan tien motion, and particularly of your bones.

This form requires a high level of awareness because, in addition to the regular lengthwise flow of chi through the structure, there is also a cross-sectional motion of energy from the entire surface of the skin into the bones that is guided by the mind-eye-heart. In Tai Chi Chi Kung we thus develop a deeper and more profound awareness in movement.

Transition to a New Direction

During Holding the Baby and the Closing Movements portion of the Tai Chi practice, move very slowly or stand still for a while so that you can really have a chance to feel the main process of working with the breath and energy centers. Draw energy in through the head, hair, crown, and torso down the legs to the soles. Concentrate on all the points in the Microcosmic Orbit: the crown, mid-eyebrow, throat point, solar plexus, navel, sexual center, perineum, sacrum, Door of Life, T11, T5/T6, C7, and Jade Pillow. All these points absorb the energy with greater strength when you direct your attention to them.

Flush the whole body with the newly collected energy so your bone marrow is cleansed throughout; your entire body is like a sponge to the external supply of chi. That is particularly true during this form, because all your skin pores are open due to your mind-eye-heart awareness.

Closing Movements

When you are ready to finish the form, smile again to your entire skeletal structure and then gather and collect chi at your navel.

14

Integrated Structure Form

The preceding forms have exposed all the aspects of the internal structure of Tai Chi Chi Kung. The Yin and Yang Form introduced the three forces and stressed the importance of relaxation for their absorption. The alignment and use of the skeletal structure given in the Rooted Form and the Chi Transfer Form give the practitioner the ability to absorb and discharge large amounts of energy and to properly maintain a connection with the heavenly and earth sources. The Tendon Activation Form teaches how the I, the combination of mind-eye-heart, moves the energy to move the body. The Tan Tien Form shows how to originate movement in the center of the body. The Healing Form makes the energy of the five directions available to their associated organs. The Skin- and Bone-Breathing Form is for absorbing chi into the bones.

The Integrated Structure Form combines all of the internal processes, both skeletal and energetic, introduced in previous chapters.

Learning to use your mind correctly is critical to becoming an accomplished Tai Chi Chi Kung practitioner. Meditations such as the Microcosmic Orbit and the Fusion of the Five Elements, in which you learn to control, condense, and direct your internal energy, are thus very important to Tai Chi Chi Kung. Students who learn only Tai Chi without any sitting meditation will find it difficult to use the mind to concentrate the energy; there are just too many things to learn at one time. It is like teaching people to draw with the left and right hands and both feet all at the same time. It just cannot be handled all at once.

A major advantage of a short form such as Tai Chi Chi Kung is that it does not take a long time to learn. Consequently, you have more time to devote to the internal work. The first goal in Tai Chi is to get the outer form right and be able to execute it automatically. Once you get the outer form down, the real work is to learn to use energy in each posture. The internal work is what is unique about Tai Chi, what distinguishes it from the external forms of martial arts. Not learning the internal aspects of Tai Chi is like having an oyster without ever bothering to look inside for the pearl.

COCKING THE BOW

The internal structure allows the body to move as a unit. A cardinal principle of Tai Chi is to lead each movement with the body, not the hands. Many people tend to move their hands first, but the legs and hips should move first and carry the rest of the body. This applies to both shifting the weight forward and sinking back.

Sinking back is very important. When you sink back, the back leg bends like a bow preparing to shoot an arrow. We call this storing energy. In Tai Chi you must store the strength inside before you release it. If this is not done properly, it is like pulling the bow back only halfway before releasing the arrow; there is then no gathering of power at all. Also, when you shift forward and back, you should try to stay level; try not to bob up and down. If you do, you will not be able to connect with the earth force.

Although this sounds simple, it seems quite difficult for some people because they are used to using their hands and arms in isolation from the rest of their bodies. When your hands move by themselves, you become tense and

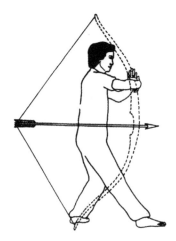

Fig. 14.1 Sinking back is like pulling a bow.   **Fig. 14.2** In stepping out, don't bounce up.

obstruct the flow of chi. When you move the whole body in a relaxed and integrated way, it feels smooth and light and yet it is also incredibly powerful. The Tai Chi classics say, "My hands do not move even half an inch [by themselves]." Elsewhere in the Tai Chi classics it says, "My hands are not my hands; my body is my hand." If you understand this, you grasp a major aspect of Tai Chi theory. Your hands are moved by your legs, spine, and tendons. While it may sometimes appear that just your hands are moving, it is really your tendons that are stretching out. This is an element of Changing the Tendons.

Because your entire upper body is stacked over your hips and legs, if your base moves, your body moves as a single controlled unit. When we use our hands and arms in isolation, eventually we segment ourselves into too many parts.

This is also true for the mind. When your mind wanders from thought to thought, it becomes weak and diffuse. You should seek to practice with one mind that rests centered in Wu Chi.

Studying Tai Chi is learning to be like a child again, in both body and mind. Children don't have much muscle, so they naturally move with structure. In this respect, a child is much more flexible than an adult who doesn't practice Tai Chi. The way of flexibility is through relaxation and by feeling delight, joy, and happiness.

ABSORBING AND DIRECTING ENERGY

Tai Chi is usually practiced slowly. The slow, even pace gives you time to really refine and perfect your structure while moving through a wide variety of postures. Once your structure is correct throughout the form, you can train your mind to manage your chi.

In Tai Chi you use your mind to gather and direct energy into your body and then to transform that energy. Once you have learned to absorb and transform energy, you can expand your awareness down, out, and up. In this way you can expand your awareness farther and farther out, connecting with the earth, heavenly, and cosmic energy, which you can then absorb and draw upon for your own use.

When you feel you can draw the energy around you, you will automatically be moving more slowly and peacefully. You feel light, joyful, and alive, and you feel the life force. In Tai Chi, the more you relax and smile to yourself, the more you get in touch with what is within you, and thus the more you feel true delight. It's not as though you have to say to yourself, "Oh, I have to practice Tai Chi again."

I have practiced Tai Chi for many years and I've come to a point where this is truly my pleasure time. I can do away with TV, with drinking, with all the so-called pleasures in life, but I cannot do away with practicing Tai Chi. Why is Tai Chi my pleasure time? Because when I practice Tai Chi, I feel delight; I am energetic and happy, and I feel my own life force.

People want to watch TV or go to nightclubs to drink and smoke because they are bored with their lives. Why are they so bored? Because they have no life force. They need something to stimulate them and give them what they think is more life force. But they have the wrong idea. Instead of gathering more chi with these activities, they are draining their chi. We call this losing-energy pleasure.

To absorb energy, it is important to start with smiling. Feel relaxed, feel joy, feel lightness inside of you. Smile to your heart. Sink down and connect to Mother Earth. Feel that you are like a tree and extend yourself up to the heavens. Open your armpits. Feel you are branching out to absorb the energy all around you.

ACHIEVING ONENESS WITH THE UNIVERSE

In the Taoist system and the Tai Chi system, the ultimate goal is to achieve oneness with the Tao, oneness with nature. In Tai Chi you reflect this in your body and mind. When you move, you move as one; everything moves at once. Instead of moving the hands first, followed by the body, followed by the legs, when you move as one your legs push you and your whole body moves simultaneously as a unit. Gradually your sense of oneness in the body will grow.

Not only does your body move in oneness, but your mind does so as well. Keep your mind and your intention completely focused on your movements. Don't allow your mind to wander and scatter into random thoughts about the past and future. Stay present. When you move forward, use your mental intention to move everything forward. When you extend your hand, extend your mind as well. Remember: "The mind leads and the chi follows; the chi leads and the body follows."

In Tai Chi we practice oneness of body, chi, and mind. When we connect to the worlds around us, below us, and above us from this inner oneness, we feel intimately connected with the universe. The Tao Te Ching says, "Carrying body and soul and embracing the one, can you avoid separation? Attending fully and becoming supple, can you be as a newborn babe?"

15

Steel Wrapped in Cotton: Martial Arts Applications

In Tai Chi there are eight forces, each of which can be used for self-defense. The forces common in self-defense applications are:

1. push down
2. push up
3. deflect to the right
4. deflect to the left
5. spiral
6. trap
7. pull backward
8. create a forward force

Each of these has practical applications in each of the eight specific movements in the Tai Chi Form:

1. Ward Off
2. Rollback
3. Press
4. Push
5. Pull Down
6. Split
7. Elbow Strike
8. Shoulder Strike

Tai Chi was originally developed as a martial art, with offensive and defensive movements. When practiced as a martial art, the degree of damage inflicted on an opponent can vary from harmless to lethal. Be aware of this as you study this chapter, and practice with great care so that you do not harm your sparring partner.

WARD OFF

There are two types of Ward Off in the Tai Chi Chi Kung Form: a yin Ward Off (a Holding the Ball application) and a yang Ward Off. Each of the eight forces named above can be used within these two aspects of Ward Off.

Fig. 15.1 Yin Ward Off

Fig. 15.2 Yang Ward Off

The Holding the Ball Ward Off is a good example of a trap. With both hands held in a receiving (yin) position, a kick or punch can be received and trapped into a locked position. Subsequently, since you have one leg free, a forward force can be generated with a kick.

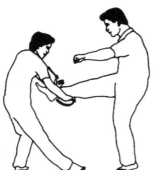

Fig. 15.3 Trapping and redirecting the opponent's kick

This is why it is so important in Tai Chi to learn to stand balanced on one leg; each time you step out and put 100 percent of the weight on one of your legs, keep in mind that your other leg is free for a sharp kick.

Fig. 15.4 Redirecting the opponent's force to the side

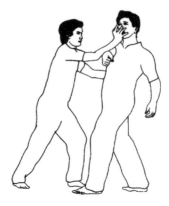

Fig. 15.5 With your right hand, push the opponent's chin to break the neck alignment. Simultaneously pull his lumbar vertebrae toward you with your left hand to break his spinal alignment.

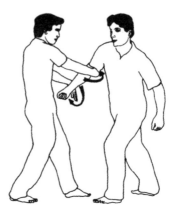

Fig. 15.6 Breaking alignment is a major goal in Tai Chi applications.

The yang Ward Off also involves trapping the force, but with a yang attack it can involve deflecting elbow to elbow and then trapping by placing one hand under the chin and the other on the spine. The Ward Off here flexes the opponent's spine unnaturally and locks him or her into submission.

In Tai Chi applications there is no need for grabbing or holding to trap with the hands when dealing with an oncoming force; a light touch with the open palms is all that is needed. This "sticky hand energy" involves a leveraging of the wrists and elbows.

In a typical attack situation, when your opponent's arm comes forward with a punch, you stick at the wrist level and apply the pull backward (keeping the opponent moving forward) at the level of the elbow. However, as in all

Fig. 15.7 Yin Ward Off: Use sticky-hand energy to break the opponent's wrist structure and elbow strength.

martial arts, an attempt at something like sticking hands in a specific area is never guaranteed, and therefore the actions are always multiple combinations to split the oncoming force in a few different directions.

Through the use of Ward Off, the force is divided into components among the eight forces mentioned. For example, you can deflect an oncoming punch to the right and at the same time trap the opponent's front leg with your own front leg. You can then follow with a short downward push and a strong upward spiraling push from the hip to finish. This is a truly a divide-and-conquer strategy.

The whole objective in Tai Chi is not to allow the oncoming force to reach you. The body is at most only about a foot or two wide, so by using the eight forces to your advantage with well-rehearsed, graceful, and coordinated body movement, what was previously a threat now becomes an application of what has been practiced in form.

Fig. 15.8 Trap the opponent's front leg with your front leg, causing his knee to lock and hyperextend.

Steel Wrapped in Cotton: Martial Arts Applications

WARD OFF COMBINATIONS

Combining Ward Off with Push or Press is done through the use of the same sequence: Ward Off, push down, and then apply Push or Press for the final assault. To protect yourself, all you need to worry about is an area around you of about one foot in diameter, to avoid an oncoming blow.

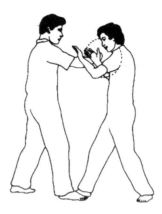

1. Gently deflect your opponent's right punch to your right

2. Once his force is neutralized, join your right palm to your left wrist

3. Guide your opponent's force downward. Absorb your opponent's force into your rear leg, gathering energy for Press.

4. Release your stored energy from your rear leg and throw him back using Press. Your front leg can attack and trap his leg simultaneously.

Steel Wrapped in Cotton: Martial Arts Applications

Fig. 15.9 Ward Off and Press

1. Use Ward Off and Push to gently stick and deflect your opponent's right-hand punch to the right side; remember not to use force: you only need his punch to miss you by a foot or so

2. As your opponent starts to retreat, begin your push with a downward movement to trap his arm against his body

3. Follow through with your Push, now directing him upward, using the spiraling force from your legs and spine

Fig. 15.10 Ward Off and Push

Fig. 15.11 Ward Off attack

ROLLBACK

In Rollback, the trapping force is used again to eliminate the oncoming punch. This is then followed by a Press and roll of the forearm on the opponent's elbow, coordinated with a spiraling force from the hips, which rotates the opponent until he goes down with his shoulder locked.

The Rollback can also be used in combination with the sinking motion to simply avoid the oncoming punch. This gentle self-defense move allows the blow to be diverted and sends the opponent past you by his own force.

A more severe application of the Rollback would be to pull the opponent down as if you were cracking a whip (his arm), to send a wave motion up the arm to the shoulder area. This would usually lodge its full force at the cervical or lumbar vertebrae, causing a great amount of irreparable damage.

The seriousness of this counterattack is similar to the one mentioned above, in which one hand is under the chin and the other is on the spine, causing an abnormal deflection of the vertebrae. The degree of damage inflicted and the seriousness of the counterattack varies from harmless to lethal in Tai Chi applications.

PRESS

Press is well illustrated by the K'an trigram of the I Ching, the Book of Changes: yang within and yin without. K'an symbolizes danger, like the proverbial wolf in sheep's clothing. In Tai Chi it is the power of steel wrapped in cotton. The outer arm stays very relaxed and sensitive while you express the force through the inner arm, making it very difficult for your opponent to feel your intention through your outer arm. The power you release from the inner arm is sudden and unexpected.

Press is applied when your opponent tries to tie up your outer arm by trapping it against your body. You move the body back to create more space and then join the back hand to the outer arm and press forward. To uproot your opponent, first apply force in a downward direction to break his root and then follow with upward force.

Another application of Press is to counter an opponent's Rollback.

PUSH

Although Push looks as if you are applying equal force with both hands, this is not the case. If you were to do that, you would be double-weighted. In Push you must remember the principles of yin and yang. When the weight is on the left leg, the left leg is yang. Therefore the right hand is your power hand, or yang hand, while the left hand is the yin, receptive and sensing, hand. Your yin hand will be feeling for your opponent's weak spot so that your yang hand will know the most vulnerable place to attack. As you shift the weight forward into the right leg, yin and yang suddenly switch; the left hand becomes yang and the right hand becomes yin. In this instance, if your opponent was mounting resistance against your right-hand attack, he may become unbalanced as your right hand suddenly becomes soft and yielding and the anticipated resistance is not there. At that same moment, you shift the attack to the left hand and push him away.

Some people think a push is not a very deadly or effective martial technique, since the opponent isn't hurt and can come right back at you. It is true that a push can be very gentle and may not hurt the opponent. In many situations, however, it may be all that is needed to cool off a hot-headed attacker. When your opponent feels how easily you are able to move him away, yet you do it without injuring him, he may sober up quickly and stop his attack.

In this day and age it is good to know martial techniques that can subdue an opponent without injury. If you don't know how to deal with an aggressor in any way other than kicking and punching, you may escalate a volatile situation unnecessarily.

All that aside, if the situation warrants a more aggressive approach, Push can be a deadly move. A quick push backed by your whole structure can cause tremendous internal damage to an opponent. The wavelike explosive force of Push can dislocate bones, rupture internal organs, and cause whiplash to the spine. In the case of multiple attackers, you can also use Push to launch one attacker against another or to hurl an opponent to the ground or against a wall or tree or down an incline. Don't underestimate the power of Push!

PULL DOWN

When your opponent punches or pushes straight at you in a horizontal direction, you redirect his force by joining with it and then steering it suddenly downward. Use all of your body weight to do this with sinking-back energy. This can cause whiplash in your opponent's neck, so be very careful about how much power you use.

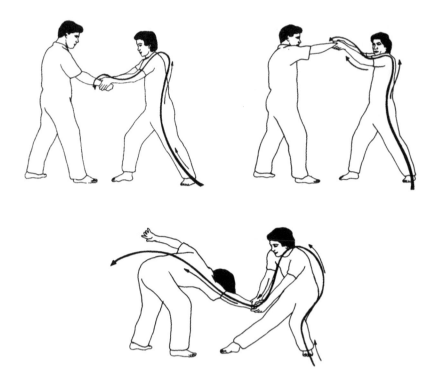

Fig. 15.12 Pull Down

SPLIT

Splitting force is used in almost every Tai Chi application. It uses the principle of divide and conquer. In general, when an opponent attacks, you want to divide his force into three directions. Your leg attacks his leg and pushes it in one direction, one of your hands guides his body in a second direction, while the other hand presses him in yet a third direction. Your opponent doesn't know which way to turn and is easily toppled.

Another application of Split divides your opponent's force in two. For example, in the sinking back between Press and Push, when your opponent tries to push you with two hands, as you sit back bring the two arms up between your opponent's two arms and expand gently outward like a wedge splitting a log. You can then counter with Push or Press, Elbow Attack, or Shoulder Strike. (See the illustrations for Shoulder Strike 2 on page 216.) Don't expand too far; you only need to make sure that your opponent's hands clear your body. Anything more is overkill and will give your opponent more opportunity to sense what you are doing and retaliate.

ELBOW ATTACK

If an opponent punches, grab his elbow, fold it, and push it up to send his force back in the reverse direction. When you do this, you can use the opponent's own elbow for leverage to strike his chin, chest, abdomen, or rib cage with the point of your elbow. You can also come in with the elbow for a more damaging counterattack.

There are approximately eighteen different elbow techniques as well as a similar number of palm techniques. An elbow attack is very powerful, especially when you know how to get all of your body weight and structure behind your elbow. You can break your opponent's rib cage due to the density of the two bones that create the elbow. Again, be careful when you attack with your elbows; you are stronger than you realize.

Fig. 15.13 Elbow Attack

SHOULDER STRIKE

The shoulder can also be used as an effective weapon against an attack. After Ward Off, if the back of the opponent's shoulder is exposed you can cup your own shoulder and launch it out against the opponent. A shoulder strike can be directed toward either the opponent's side or his middle.

1. Deflect opponent's attack to the right

2. Attack his chest with your right shoulder

Fig. 15.14 Shoulder Strike 1

This type of attack should be done by rounding the scapulae, which prevents the shock of the contact from doing damage to you. If your opponent's arms are up, leaving his sides exposed, a slight sinking motion can allow you to hit your shoulder against the opponent's rib cage or sternum. Your entire weight is directed from the ground to the hip to the shoulder, which creates a head-on collision between the corner of your shoulder and a vulnerable area on the opponent.

1. Split your opponent's force

2. Attack his sternum with your shoulder

Steel Wrapped in Cotton: Martial Arts Applications

Fig. 15.15 Shoulder Strike 2

People often fall into the trap of thinking that our hands and feet are our only weapons. With Tai Chi, always remember that the entire body is your weapon. If an opponent grabs your wrist or elbow, relax; let him have your hand while you fold up your arm and attack with your shoulder. A shoulder strike can crack bones, dislocate joints, and knock an opponent unconscious.

SINKING FORCE

Sinking back is very important in providing effective strength to your counter-attacks; otherwise it is like pulling the bow back only halfway before releasing an arrow. In Tai Chi, gather your strength within until you have to let it go. The restriction leads to a controlled, directed, and more powerful attack. The entire basis for the sinking force is to connect with the earth to give strength to your attack. Therefore it is important not to bob up and down; if you do, you will be unable to connect with the earth force.

The illustrations here show a partner exercise for Sinking Force training.

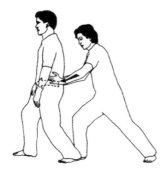

1. Have your partner push your hips from behind

2. Sink your weight down into your rear leg and push back with the force of your front leg

3. Sinking Force provdies the power in Pull Down

Fig. 15.16 Partner exercise for Sinking Force training

SINGLE WHIP

Single Whip can be viewed as a means of spreading out the forces of an attack from both hands in sequence. At first the Crane's Beak is used to stick to the wrist of the opponent's first attack (on the same side as the beak). The beak is used to deflect that hand to the side by hooking over from the outside and pulling it out and away.

Next, in the Reaching Up to Heaven motion, the inside of the other wrist deflects the opponent's second attack from the inside, deflecting it out and away. At this point the opponent is standing with his arms apart, vulnerable to an array of attacks on his midsection.

Single Whip is so named because it can actually be used as a whip. Following a Ward Off, the beak can be whipped into action to "peck" at the opponent's trapezius, for example. This is very painful to the opponent when you can relax and put all your weight and force into the tiny point of the beak.

1. Deflect your opponent's punch with Crane's Beak to your right

2. Deflect his right punch to your left with Reaching to Heaven

Fig. 15.17 Single Whip application

3. Hook his front leg and pull it toward you

4. Push his chin back with Single-Hand Push

Fig. 15.18 Single Whip attack

The beak can also be used to go into vulnerable pressure points on the surface of the opponent's body, such as between the joints and vertebrae. The throat center and groin are also lethal areas to attack with the beak.

CUTTING LEG

You learn Cutting Leg from the Tai Chi Walk. You may have a chance to cut an opponent's leg because he has to defend all three areas of his body: upper, middle, and lower. This may be beyond his level of awareness and ability. Your shin needs to be toughened to properly apply this move so that you do not cause yourself pain. If you are cutting from the front it will be shin against shin, and the stronger shin will succeed.

For the front Cutting Leg, step behind the opponent's forward foot, turn the foot up on the heel, hook around the back of the opponent's leg, and cut down by twisting his ankle with your shin. This can be done from the inside or the outside of the leg.

The Tai Chi masters use this cutting technique to wage a dual-pronged attack, one above and the other below. Cutting Leg can be used on virtually every step of attack and counterattack during a confrontation.

Fig. 15.19 Cutting Leg attack

INCORPORATING APPLICATIONS INTO THE TAI CHI FORM

As you practice Tai Chi by yourself, envision yourself using each of the applications described in this chapter in self-defense. This is why Tai Chi is often called shadowboxing. This enhances the more practical side of protecting yourself with Tai Chi as well as creates an awareness of directing the energy, making the Tai Chi moves much more effective during practical application.

Dance of the Tao

Taoism is a way of life that can be expressed through Tai Chi. Tai Chi practice combines the working development of body, mind, and energy by finding balance and coordination between these aspects of our being. However, the Tao does not stop when practice has ended. The same process of harmonizing body, mind, and energy must continue into daily life.

The emphasis in Tai Chi practice is on creating oneness within oneself and between oneself and the Tao. Here are some principles to follow in bringing the Tao into your daily awareness.

Move as a Whole

Moving with the chi force and allowing it to move with you enables you to absorb and combine the external energy with the life force. At this level, oneness with the Tao begins as you learn to move your body in an integrated way. Chi is brought into harmony with the body through sensitization.

There is an inherent wholeness to the movements of animals, whereas for people, aspects of our being tend to become separated: hands from legs, mind from body, body from spirit. This can be seen when people tense their muscles and wind up hurting themselves when they try to lift, pull, or push things. This is because they do not use their bodies in an integrated way. Their mind, hands, legs, and back all work separately, resulting in back injuries, torn knees, and dislocated shoulders.

Be Aware in Your Movements

Awareness in movement is very important in Tai Chi practice. People commonly disassociate their minds and their bodies, often doing one thing while the mind is thinking of something completely different.

In Tai Chi we focus on the most minute details of how we move, breathe, and use our mental intention. With regular practice, this kind of awareness begins to spill over into daily life. Through this increased awareness in practice, the dangers of ordinary-life injuries, mistakes, and accidents are greatly reduced.

Feel One with Nature

Division is the sign of our times, whether that be separation by country of origin, cultural heritage, ethnic custom or religion, sex, age, race, or economic status. As a result, we see ourselves as separate from nature and imagine we can despoil the environment without doing any harm to ourselves. We must realize that we can continue to exist only by living in harmony and balance with the universe and with nature.

Bees pollinate, bacteria recycle degradable material, and worms restore the earth for further growth. Every being has its role to play in nature; without each part of nature, only a mountain of death would exist. Everything from trees to stones has its function in nature, and yet we allow ourselves to become alienated from the ground of our own being.

The movement of the Tao is a continuous flow from yin to yang—the day flows into the night, the sun cycles with the moon, and the winter yields to the summer. All these aspects of nature participate in an endless cycle, keeping the universe in balance. This we can experience through the practice of Tai Chi.

Know the Tao

The Tao is the way of living in harmony with nature and the universe that has guided Chinese civilization for five thousand years. But the only way to realize practical benefits from the Tao is to cultivate and practice it. To put it simply, "If you do it, you get it; if you don't do it, you don't get it!" The Tao is more than just a philosophy or an intellectual exercise. It is truly a whole way of living. The various levels of practice, if fully implemented, can provide enjoyment, happiness, and fulfillment.

Tai Chi Chi Kung is an integral part of the Tao, the dance of yin and yang.

Dance of the Tao

All the principles of the Tao are present within Tai Chi Chi Kung practice. Practice daily and you will gradually become an embodiment of the Tao. Balance, harmony, and integrity will be present in everything you do; you will begin to move through life with Wu Wei, effortlessness—not doing, yet leaving nothing undone.

Appendix 1

Energetic Preparations for Tai Chi Chi Kung

INNER SMILE

The Inner Smile is a powerful relaxation and self-healing technique that uses the energy of happiness and love as a language to communicate with the internal organs of the body. A genuine smile transmits loving energy that has the power to calm, balance, and heal.

When you smile inwardly to the organs and glands, your whole body feels loved and appreciated. The Inner Smile begins at the eyes and mid-eyebrow point. The eyes are connected to the autonomic nervous system, which in turn is connected to all the muscles, organs, and glands. As one of the first parts of the body to receive signals, the eyes cause the organs and glands to accelerate activity at times of stress or danger and to slow down when a crisis has passed. When the eyes relax, they activate the parasympathetic nervous system and cause the rest of the body to relax.

As you activate the loving energy, you will feel the energy of the Inner Smile flow down the entire length of the body like a waterfall. This is a very powerful and effective tool to counteract stress and tension.

There are three vital aspects to each phase of the Inner Smile. First, direct the awareness to a specific part of the body. Second, smile to that part of the body; send it a genuine feeling of love, gratitude, and appreciation for its role in keeping the body running smoothly and in good health. Third, feel that part of the body relax and smile back to you.

The Inner Smile Practice

1. Stand in Wu Chi stance or sit on the edge of a chair with the hands comfortably clasped together and resting on the lap. Keep the eyes closed and breathe normally. Follow the breathing until it becomes smooth, quiet, deep, even, calm, and soft.

2. Relax the forehead. Imagine yourself in one of your favorite beautiful places in the world. Recall the sights, sounds, and sensations of that place until they are vividly in your mind's eye. Then imagine suddenly meeting someone you love. Picture him or her smiling lovingly and radiantly at you. Feel yourself basking in the warmth of that smile like sunshine, drawing it into your eyes. Feel the eyes relaxing and responding with a smile of their own.

3. Picture the healing chi of nature—the fresh energy of waterfalls, mountains, and oceans—as a golden cloud of benevolent loving energy in front of you. We call this the Higher Human Plane energy of the atmosphere, the blended chi of heaven and earth, or the Cosmic Particle force. Direct the smiling energy in the eyes to this Cosmic Particle energy around you, drawing it into the mid-eyebrow point. Feel the brow relaxing and widening. Spiral the energy into the mid-eyebrow point; feel it amplifying the power of your smile.

4. Let the smiling awareness flow down over the cheeks, down through the jaw muscles and tongue, and down through the neck and throat, soothing and relaxing as it goes.

5. Smile down to the thymus gland and the heart. Feel them open like flowers in the morning with love, joy, and happiness bubbling out of them.

6. Smile down to the rest of the solid organs: lungs, liver, pancreas, spleen, kidneys, sexual organs, and reproductive system. Thank each of them for their work in keeping you vibrant and healthy. This completes the first line of the Inner Smile.

7. Return your awareness to your eyes and recharge the energy of your smile. Then draw in more of the golden light of the Cosmic Particle force.

8. Roll the tongue around the mouth until you have gathered some saliva. Smile to the saliva and draw the smiling energy and the golden light into the saliva, transforming it into a healing nectar.

9. Swallow the saliva in two or three strong gulps. Follow it with awareness down the esophagus, smiling as it goes, feeling the healing nectar soothing and refreshing the esophagus. Continue smiling through the rest of the digestive tract: the stomach, small intestine, gall bladder, large intestine,

rectum, anus, bladder, and urethra. Thank these organs for their work in giving you energy through ingestion, digestion, absorption, and elimination. This completes the second or middle line of the Inner Smile.

10. Return your awareness to your eyes and recharge your smile. Then once again connect with the golden light of the Cosmic Particle force.

11. Now smile to the brain, to the left and right hemispheres, and to the pituitary, thalamus, and pineal glands. Then smile down through the spinal column vertebra by vertebra, thanking each vertebra for its work in protecting the spinal cord and supporting the skeletal structure. This completes the third or back line of the Inner Smile.

12. Return your awareness to your eyes once again and recharge your smiling energy.

13. Smile down through the whole body, particularly to any places that feel tired, sore, painful, weak, empty, or tense. Shower these parts with the healing nectar of your smiling awareness.

14. Finally, smile to the navel and collect the energy there.

15. Starting in the center of the navel, begin spiraling the energy outward. Men should spiral the energy in a clockwise direction, making thirty-six revolutions; women spiral the energy in a counterclockwise direction, also making thirty-six revolutions. Take care not to make the outer ring of the spiral any larger than a grapefruit; circling above the diaphragm causes too much energy to flow into the heart and overstimulates the emotions, whereas circling below the pubic bone sends too much energy into the reproductive system, where it may be lost through ejaculation or menses. After completing the first set of revolutions, spiral inward in the opposite direction twenty-four times, ending at the center of the navel.

MICROCOSMIC ORBIT MEDITATION

The Microcosmic Orbit Meditation awakens, circulates, and directs chi through the Governor Channel, which ascends from the base of the spine to the crown, and the Functional Channel (also called the Conception Vessel), which runs down the front midline of the body. Dedicated practice of this ancient esoteric method eliminates stress and nervous tension, energizes the internal organs, restores health to damaged tissues, and establishes a peaceful sense of well-being.

The meditations of the Microcosmic Orbit system also strengthen the Original Chi and teach you the basics of circulating chi. They allow the palms, the soles of the feet, the mid-eyebrow point, and the crown to open. These specific locations are the major points at which energy can be absorbed, condensed, and transformed into fresh new life force.

The Tai Chi classics say, "The mind moves and the Chi follows." When you focus your attention at a specific place in the body, you automatically activate the chi at that place. By the mere act of attention, you consciously link the brain to the local sensory receptors at that place. The nervous system in turn creates local changes in capillary circulation, muscle activity, and lymphatic flow.

All the movements in these systems require energy; we call this energy chi. The sensations of these energetic changes can be subtle or dramatic. They are characterized by such feelings as warmth, tingling, pulsing, expansion, vibration, and effervescence. You may sense one or more of these feelings depending on your level of sensitivity and your experience with meditation and Chi Kung. Don't worry if you feel little or nothing at first; just focus your attention at each point. Whether you feel it or not, your chi will be moving. With practice, you will begin to feel the chi moving more vividly.

Spend at least one week concentrating on completing the Microcosmic Orbit before proceeding to learn the Tai Chi Chi Kung form. Read through the books *Awaken Healing Energy Through the Tao* and *Awaken Healing Light of the Tao*, paying special attention to the question-and-answer sections.

Basic Microcosmic Orbit Meditation Practice

1. Begin your meditation practice with the Inner Smile. As you did for the Inner Smile, stand in Wu Chi stance or sit on the edge of a chair with your hands comfortably clasped together and resting on the lap. Keep the eyes closed and breathe normally. Follow the breathing until it becomes smooth, quiet, deep, even, calm, and soft. Smile down to the front, middle, and back lines to relax and harmonize the body, breath, and mind. Then smile to the lower tan tien, but do not collect energy yet.

2. Activate the Original Chi in the lower tan tien. Focus your attention on the tan tien, breathing naturally using lower abdominal breathing. Use your intention to create a feeling of warmth in the lower tan tien. Feel it as the reservoir of your Original Chi, the main battery of your entire energetic system. Imagine that each breath is like a bellows fanning the fire in the lower tan tien. Hold your awareness there until you feel the lower tan tien filled with chi.

3. Begin to move the energy in the Functional Channel. Move the awareness to the navel and concentrate there until you feel that the energy

has gathered at that point. Then bring the attention to the sexual center (Sperm/Ovary Palace). When you feel sufficient energy gathered there, proceed in a similar way to the perineum (Gate of Life and Death).

4. Direct the energy through the Governor Channel. When you have accumulated substantial energy at each point, move the awareness to the next successive point. From the perineum, continue concentrating the energy at each point up the spine to the head: to the coccyx, the sacral hiatus, the Door of Life, T11, the Jade Pillow, the crown, and the mid-eyebrow point (the third eye).

5. Now connect the two channels. Bring the attention to the tip of the tongue. Touch the tip of the tongue to the palate, connecting the two main channels of the Microcosmic Orbit. Press and release the tongue against the palate nine to thirty-six times. This activates the palate point and enables the energy to flow down the Functional Channel.

6. Complete the circulation in the Functional Channel. Direct the attention to each point along the Functional Channel: to the throat center, the heart center, the solar plexus, and back to the navel. This completes one cycle of the Microcosmic Orbit. You may notice less sensation in the Functional Channel because there are seven parallel pathways along which the energy may descend, and thus the energy may become more diffuse.

7. Continue to circulate energy through the Microcosmic Orbit. Circulate energy through the entire cycle at least nine times. As you gain experience you can increase the number of circulations to 36, 72, 108, or 360. At some point you may feel the energy begin to move by itself. This is a good sign; if it happens, don't try to restrain it, just let it flow at its own pace.

⟳ Connect to the Chi of Heaven, Earth, and Man

1. Once you have opened the Microcosmic Orbit, open the soles of the feet to the earth and allow the earth energy to ascend the legs to the perineum to join the Microcosmic Orbit. Use the mind's eye to perceive this energy as a cool blue light.

2. When the energy reaches the top of the head, open the crown point to receive the heavenly force and join it with the Microcosmic Orbit. You may experience this as a warm violet light coming from the North Star.

3. When the energy reaches the mid-eyebrow point, relax the brow and reconnect with the Cosmic Particle force you experienced during the Inner Smile. Allow this golden light to join with the Microcosmic Orbit.

4. When you are finished, guide the energy back to the navel and collect it

by spiraling it thirty-six times outward and twenty-four times inward, as at the end of the Inner Smile.

It takes some people longer than others to complete the Microcosmic Orbit, depending on their level of energy, their general state of health, the number of obstructions in the channels, and how long it takes to clear each obstruction.

If after two weeks you have not completed the entire Microcosmic Orbit successfully, reverse the energy flow one center at a time, starting from the last point you have reached.

Spend more time at the Door of Life. Then bring the energy down to the perineum and down the backs of the legs to the Kidney 1 points at the soles of the feet (Bubbling Springs). Then, proceeding up along the inner sides of the legs, return to the perineum.

Now continue up to the sexual center, then to the navel, and then up to the solar plexus. Spend one week concentrating on the solar plexus point.

Proceed to the heart point and spend one week concentrating there. Then advance to the throat point and spend one week there.

This process will open up the Functional Channel. Once you have opened the Functional Channel, bring the energy to the tip of the tongue, thereby connecting this route with the Governor Channel. Your Microcosmic Orbit should now be running properly. If not, concentrate on any points along the spine that feel obstructed, spending one week at each point. If you do this, you should be assured of success.

IRON SHIRT CHI KUNG STANDING MEDITATION

Iron Shirt Chi Kung is one of the martial arts aspects of the Universal Tao system. It is also an important foundation for both healing and spiritual work. Iron Shirt Chi Kung develops internal power and a well-conditioned body through simple techniques that build and store chi. These techniques also help you become rooted to the earth's energy, which keeps the body centered and balanced.

There are many aspects to Iron Shirt Chi Kung training. Here we present only the basics needed in your practice of Tai Chi Chi Kung.

To fully master Iron Shirt, you must study with a qualified instructor. You may also refer to the Universal Tao books *Iron Shirt Chi Kung* and *Bone Marrow Nei Kung*.

 Basic Iron Shirt Chi Kung: Embracing the Tree

1. Stand with your feet parallel, knee-to-toe-length apart. Bend your knees slightly as if crouching. Gently twist the legs outward as though they were screwing into the ground. Tilt the sacrum and tailbone forward until you feel the feet press firmly into the ground. Round the scapulae, relax the chest, and hold the head erect. Position the arms as if they were encircling a tree, keeping the elbows sunk. Point the thumbs upward, point the rest of the fingers toward the corresponding fingers on the other hand, and gently stretch the fingers apart until the tendons have become taut but not tense. Keep the weight balanced over the Bubbling Spring points of the feet. Feel the whole skeletal structure in perfect alignment with gravity.

2. Allow the body to rock slightly forward and back and side to side to open to the earth energy rising up.

3. Practice Bellows Breathing: As you inhale, press the diaphragm down and expand the lower abdomen, sides, and back at waist level. As you exhale, raise the diaphragm and pull the abdomen in. Take about one second for each complete breath (in and out). Perform eighteen to thirty-six times.

4. Practice all the stages of the Microcosmic Orbit in this position. If the arms feel tired, lower them but maintain the circle structure of the arms.

5. Practice Bone Breathing and Marrow Washing as outlined in chapter 13.

6. Conclude by collecting energy at the navel.

Appendix 2
Tai Chi Physiology

The ancient Chinese martial art of Tai Chi was developed through years of experience and practice. In the West, however, with the advances of science, many question the basis for the vast increase in power that can be achieved through the practice. In response to those who insist, "Show me, I'm from Missouri," we include the beginnings of a scientific investigation that has been provided by Albert L. Chan, Ph.D. Dr. Chan has practiced and studied Tai Chi Chi Kung and Taoist meditation for fourteen years with Master Chia. He has also studied Wing Tsun Chuan for twelve years. He holds a Ph.D. degree in physics and a master's degree in computer science. Dr. Chan is currently researching the physics of sport. He is particularly interested in analyzing the martial arts and sports.

INNER STRUCTURE

The human skeleton is effectively a biomechanical power transporter. Mechanical power can be transferred from one end of the system to the other, provided that all the involved components are in proper alignment (which is why we discuss structure so often in Tai Chi training). Tai Chi has developed from the study of the coordination and structure of movement, such that the power from the legs can be transported to the pelvis, to the base of the spine, to each vertebra of the spine, to the scapulae, and ultimately through the forearms and hands. The ultimate goal is self-defense. Poor posture or improper alignment restricts the flow of this power.

Because the legs, which generate the power, have the strongest and largest muscles in the human body, the force they can transmit to the attacking arm is tremendous. This force can be used to throw opponents many feet away or to incapacitate an opponent by exerting a powerful push or punch.

The Tai Chi form evolved as a way in which energy from specific power points in the body could be directed and focused through the use of structure. By carefully training each part of the body to perform only a few functions, the techniques that were developed are relatively easy to master.

The forward and backward directions of motion and balance are controlled by both legs, since they are the power source. The hips control the rotational motion of the entire upper torso as well as the legs. This force plays a particularly important role in using the circular action to redirect an opponent's attack. When a direct force is encountered, rather then requiring the power to both overcome and redirect the force, the circular action uses the oncoming power of the attack and follows it through by deflecting it away from the body.

The spine transfers the power from the hips to the scapulae through its ability to twist and flex in a controlled and supple way. An unnaturally twisted or curved spine reduces the amount of power that can be transferred. The scapulae control the flow of this power and the movement of both arms through a careful positioning relative to the spine. When the hips, spine, and scapulae move as one unit, an integrated strength is created that is more powerful than any of its individual components.

The arms are used to feel the approaching force of the opponent and to begin the process of partially receiving and partially deflecting this power accordingly.

All the parts of the body should be relaxed so that the oncoming force can be sensed and reacted to without resistance. A tensed arm or shoulder increases reaction time and simultaneously reduces the efficient transfer of power through the body, thus allowing less of the oncoming force to flow through the structure. On the other hand, a relaxed body produces an increase in the amount of power being generated.

A good example of this is a simple push. The structure collects power from the legs as they are pressing into the ground, from the hips as they rotate, from the spine as it flexes, and from the shoulders as they extend. At each point the total power increases as it is directed up the body to the attacking arm or shoulder. The amount of power that reaches the pushing hand or fist is much greater than that which is being produced just at the legs.

The structure is also used as a lever to deflect or divert an opponent's powerful blow or push. A powerful oncoming push can either be redirected to another direction (deflection) or absorbed to a great extent by the structure through the spine and down the legs, where it diverts into the ground, leaving the practitioner unharmed. This is the essence of rooting. The proper alignment of the structure of the body provides a path for this great power to flow through while providing additional energy to other points of the body for a counterattack.

TAI CHI CHI KUNG FORM

There are eight basic movements in Tai Chi: Ward Off, Rollback, Press, Push, Pull Down, Split, Elbow Strike, and Shoulder Strike. When the basic principles are understood and applied, the practitioner can employ other, equally effective techniques.

Tai Chi uses gravity and the leverage of the legs for pulling the opponent off balance. An important aspect of the practice is avoiding moving one's center of gravity up and down, which would waste a considerable amount of energy and would interfere with a smooth structural motion.

The structure of the Tai Chi practitioner acts like a rubber ball. The harder you strike it, the more it yields (sinking) and the more force it returns to the opponent by bouncing back. Ultimately the ball has the advantage, because the attacker becomes exhausted as his attacking force is absorbed.

TENDONS

Holding correct Tai Chi posture implies using the minimal amount of energy to withstand the maximum oncoming force. Furthermore, a good posture in Tai Chi uses the tendons instead of the muscles for proper rooting and power.

In a Rollback movement to the left, as the practitioner turns the hip to the left, the left thigh is being led in the same direction. Since the left foot is stationary on the ground and the knee is virtually a hinge joint (cannot be twisted rotationally), the length of the left leg is twisted, which in turn wraps the leg tendons around the bones. As a result, these tendons are stretched.

The tendons are flexible and elastic. They can store energy by stretching and winding like a rubber band. The Achilles tendons in particular, which are located at the ankles, are the largest tendons in the human body and are capable of storing the energy of a 1,000-pound pull. The Rollback to the left stores a considerable amount of energy in the left leg tendons. The stored energy is then released back to the body as the left leg unwinds and turns the body into the Press posture. The energy is thus stored or gathered in the Rollback and released in the Press. This is true of almost all the yin-to-yang transitions in the Tai Chi form.

The tendons act like springs. A correct posture can absorb and redirect force like a spring in a car's suspension. In a sense the tendons conserve and recycle energy that would otherwise be wasted.

A similar technique is used by a baseball pitcher, who winds up his body and hips to the extreme before throwing the baseball. Likewise, in most other martial arts, the body is fully torqued prior to throwing the kick or punch. However, with Tai Chi the key advantage is through the extensive use of tendon power.

This use of tendon power can be found throughout the Tai Chi form. For instance, in the right-hand Single Whip movement, the standing leg (right) is twisted approximately 40 degrees or more, with the foot remaining flat and stationary on the ground. Energy is stored in the leg tendons, which is then released to help the body unwind and execute the strike with the right hand by extending the beak.

To illustrate the point, one can hold the right-hand Single Whip posture and not perform the strike. If the practitioner then lifts up the left leg so that it does not touch the ground, the right leg naturally unwinds and releases the stored energy to turn the body to the left.

The tendons are also used to absorb and rebound the power from an opponent's push. When a practitioner is being pushed at the hands while in a Press posture, the force travels from the hand to the elbow and part of that energy is used to stretch the triceps tendon. The rest of the force travels to the shoulders, which also consume part of the energy through the tendons around the scapulae. As the residual force is transmitted down the spine and to the back of the leg, energy is absorbed along the tendons that help support these areas. All excess force is then transmitted into the ground through the nine points of the feet. When the opponent's power has been absorbed in this manner, the practitioner can release this stored energy along with his or her own additional muscle power, yielding a much more powerful counter. A returned Press can either throw the opponent off balance or lift him up and project him several feet away.

RESEARCH

In recent research on runners, it has been confirmed that leg tendons (especially the Achilles tendons) increase the efficiency of running. Tendons absorb the energy of landing and release it for the subsequent push from the ground. If the tendons were not elastic, the runner would require three times the energy to run the same distance.

Appendix 2

This effect is more apparent on four-legged animals such as horses and camels. Their lower legs consist mainly of tendons, which maximize the efficiency of running and conserving energy.

Furthermore, my doctoral dissertation proves that on account of their elasticity, the tendons of the hand increase the maximum speed of a forward punch by as much as 6 percent, which is equivalent to a 12 percent increase in impact power.

CONCLUSIONS

Tai Chi uses correct posture to distribute energy to the entire body, to redirect force, and to pass force to the ground. On demand, the structure collects energy from the tendons and muscles and focuses it to a point for striking.

Besides the awesome power that Tai Chi can control, it promotes good physical health because of the exercise provided to the spine, hips, legs, and arms and their associated tendons, muscles, and joints. It also trains the mind to develop a vital life force (called chi) within the body. The physical and mental exercises enhance one another to bring long life to the practitioner.

Tai Chi is an art that applies the fundamentals of movement and body structure. Tai Chi focuses and channels power within the body for the purpose of self-defense, which is then expressed optimally in terms of the efficient use of energy.

Bibliography

Chia, Mantak. *Awaken Healing Light of the Tao*, Huntington, N.Y.: Healing Tao Books, 1993.

———. *Bone Marrow Nei Kung*. Huntington, N.Y.: Healing Tao Books, 1989.

———. *Chi Nei Tsang: Internal Organs Chi Massage*. Huntington, N.Y.: Healing Tao Books, 1990.

———. *Fusion of the Five Elements I*. Huntington, N.Y.: Healing Tao Books, 1989.

———. *Iron Shirt Chi Kung I*. Huntington, N.Y.: Healing Tao Books, l986.

———. *Taoist Ways to Transform Stress into Vitality*. Huntington, N.Y.: Healing Tao Books, 1985.

Chia, Mantak, and Michael Winn. *Taoist Secrets of Love: Cultivating Male Sexual Energy*. Santa Fe: Aurora Press, 1984.

Cleary, Thomas, trans. *The Taoist I Ching*. Boston: Shambhala, 1986.

Horwitz, Tem, and Susan Kimmelman, with H. H. Lui. *T'ai Chi Ch'uan: The Technique of Power*. Chicago: Chicago Review Press, 1976.

Lee, Ying-Arng. *Lee's Modified Tai Chi Chuan for Health*. Hong Kong: Unicorn Press, 1968.

Liao, Waysun. *Tai Chi Classics*. Boston and London: Shambhala, 1990.

Lo, Benjamin Pang Jeng, with Martin Inn, Robert Amacker, and Susan Foe (translators and editors). *The Essence of Tai Chi Ch'uan: The Literary Tradition*. Richmond, CA: North Atlantic Books, 1979.

Jou, Tsung Hwa. *Imagination Becomes Reality: The Teachings of Master T. T. Liang*. St. Cloud, Minn.: Bubbling Well Press, 1986.

———, with Stuart Alve Olson (compiler) and Gerald Kuehl (editor). *The Tao of Tai-Chi Chuan*. Rutland, Vt.: Charles E. Tuttle Co., 1980.

Wang Peisheng, and Zeng Weiqi. *Wu Style Taijiquan*. Hong Kong: Hai Feng Publishing Company, 1983.

 About the Authors

MANTAK CHIA has been studying the Taoist approach to life since child-hood. His mastery of this ancient knowledge, enhanced by his study of other disciplines, has resulted in the development of the Universal Tao System, which is now being taught throughout the world.

Mantak Chia was born in Thailand to Chinese parents in 1944. When he was six years old, he learned from Buddhist monks how to sit and "still the mind." While in grammar school, he learned traditional Thai boxing, and soon went on to acquire considerable skill in Aikido, Yoga, and Tai Chi. His studies of the Taoist way of life began in earnest when he was a student in Hong Kong, ultimately leading to his mastery of a wide variety of esoteric disciplines. To better understand the mechanisms behind healing energy, he also studied Western anatomy and medical sciences.

Master Chia has taught his system of healing and energizing practices to tens of thousands of students and trained more than two thousand instructors and practitioners throughout the world. He has established centers for Taoist study and training in many countries around the globe. In June 1990 he was honored by the International Congress of Chinese Medicine and Qi Gong (Chi Kung), which named him the Qi Gong Master of the Year.

JUAN LI was born in Havana, Cuba. He began his Taoist studies in 1965 with a comparative study of the Tao Te Ching in English translations and majored in Chinese studies at Brooklyn College.

In 1982, Juan Li began his study of the traditional Taoist internal energy formulas with Master Mantak Chia. He went on to become a senior instructor in the Universal Tao System, and today he spends the greater part of his time presenting these teachings in Western Europe. Juan Li lives in Spain with his wife, Renu, who is also a senior Universal Tao instructor.

The Universal Tao System and Training Center

THE UNIVERSAL TAO SYSTEM

The ultimate goal of Taoist practice is to transcend physical boundaries through the development of the soul and the spirit within the human. That is also the guiding principle behind the Universal Tao, a practical system of self-development that enables individuals to complete the harmonious evolution of their physical, mental, and spiritual bodies. Through a series of ancient Chinese meditative and internal energy exercises, the practitioner learns to increase physical energy, release tension, improve health, practice self-defense, and gain the ability to heal himself and others. In the process of creating a solid foundation of health and well-being in the physical body, the practitioner also creates the basis for developing his or her spiritual potential by learning to tap into the natural energies of the sun, moon, earth, stars, and other environmental forces.

The Universal Tao practices are derived from ancient techniques rooted in the processes of nature. They have been gathered and integrated into a coherent, accessible system for well-being that works directly with the life force, or chi, that flows through the meridian system of the body.

Master Chia has spent years developing and perfecting techniques for teaching these traditional practices to students around the world through ongoing classes, workshops, private instruction, and healing sessions, as well as books and video and audio products. Further information can be obtained at www.universal-tao.com.

THE UNIVERSAL TAO TRAINING CENTER

The Tao Garden Resort and Training Center in northern Thailand is the home of Master Chia and serves as the worldwide headquarters for Universal Tao activities. This integrated wellness, holistic health, and training center is situated on eighty acres surrounded by the beautiful Himalayan foothills near the historic walled city of Chiang Mai. The serene setting includes flower and herb gardens ideal for meditation, open-air pavilions for practicing Chi Kung, and a health and fitness spa.

The center offers classes year-round, as well as summer and winter retreats. It can accommodate two hundred students, and group leasing can be arranged. For more information, you may fax the center at (66) (53) 495-852, or e-mail universaltao@universal-tao.com.

The Universal
Tao System
and Training
Center

Index

BOOKS OF RELATED INTEREST

Healing Light of the Tao
Foundational Practices to Awaken Chi Energy
by Mantak Chia

The Inner Smile
Increasing Chi through the Cultivation of Joy
by Mantak Chia

Wisdom Chi Kung
Practices for Enlivening the Brain with Chi Energy
by Mantak Chia

Iron Shirt Chi Kung
by Mantak Chia

Tan Tien Chi Kung
Foundational Exercises for Empty Force and Perineum Power
by Mantak Chia

The Secret Teachings of the Tao Te Ching
by Mantak Chia and Tao Huang

Energy Balance through the Tao
Exercises for Cultivating Yin Energy
by Mantak Chia

Chi Self-Massage
The Taoist Way of Rejuvenation
by Mantak Chia

Inner Traditions • Bear & Company
P.O. Box 388
Rochester, VT 05767
1-800-246-8648
www.InnerTraditions.com

Or contact your local bookseller